D1236732

Materialism

Materialism
Terry Eagleton

YALE UNIVERSITY PRESS
NEW HAVEN AND LONDON

For information about this and other Yale University Press publications, please contact:
U.S. Office: sales.press@yale.edu   yalebooks.com
Europe Office: sales@yaleup.co.uk   yalebooks.co.uk

Typeset in Adobe Garamond Pro by IDSUK (DataConnection) Ltd
Printed in the United States of America

Library of Congress Cataloging-in-Publication Data

Names: Eagleton, Terry, 1943- author.
Title: Materialism / Terry Eagleton.
Description: New Haven : Yale University Press. | Includes bibliographical
    references.
Identifiers: LCCN 2016025877 | ISBN 9780300218800 (cl : alk. paper)
Subjects: LCSH: Materialism.
Classification: LCC B825 .E24 2017 | DDC 146/.3—dc23
LC record available at https://lccn.loc.gov/2016025877

A catalogue record for this book is available from the British Library.

10 9 8 7 6 5 4 3 2 1

In memory of Leo Pyle

Contents

Preface

THIS IS AMONG other things a book about the body, but not (such, anyway, is my fervent hope) the kind of body that is currently fashionable in cultural studies, and which as a subject of discussion has become narrow, exclusivist and tediously repetitive. There is, then, a polemical subtext to the study, as it seeks to examine modes of human creatureliness which postmodern orthodoxy has largely shoved to the sidelines, and which are among other things true of all human bodies regardless of, say, gender and ethnicity. I trust that this unabashed universalism will prove sufficiently scandalous to the commissars of contemporary cultural discourse.

It would seem that those postgraduate students around the globe these days who are not working on vampires or graphic novels are at work on the body, but in ways that exclude certain productive approaches to it. As usual, those who sing the praises of inclusivity are remarkably ignorant of just how much their own favoured idiom leaves out. Cultural studies is concerned for the most part with the ethnic, gendered, queer, starving, constructed, ageing, bedecked, disabled, cybernetic, bio-political body – the body as object of the sexual gaze, locus of pleasure or pain, inscribed with power, discipline or desire. The human body dealt with in this book, by contrast, is of a more rudimentary kind. It is not in the first place a cultural construct. What is said of it applies as much in Cambodia as in Cheltenham, as much to Belgian females as to Sri Lankan males. If it is true of Hillary Clinton, it was equally true of Cicero. Only those postmodern dogmatists for whom, astonishingly, all universal claims are oppressive, with the exception of that particular universal claim, are likely to be scandalised by such an approach.

Cultural studies has produced some valuable insights into the body, but seems to be unaware of its own rather depressing political history in this respect. One of the chief sources of the topic is the work of Michel Foucault, whose writing also marks a crisis of the revolutionary left in the wake of the late 1960s. It was at the point when certain more ambitious forms of radical politics seemed to have faltered, rebuffed by powerful right-wing forces, that historical materialism began to give way to cultural materialism, and an interest in the body started to gather strength. If it served to challenge a leftist politics too cerebrally remote from the senses, it also had a hand in displacing it. Like any fetish, then, this particular body serves to plug a gap. The relation between the body and socialist politics was kept on the political agenda by some pioneering currents of feminism; but by the 1980s talk of socialism was yielding ground to talk of sexuality, and a cultural left that was now for the most part shamefacedly silent on the subject of capitalism was growing increasingly vociferous on the question of corporeality. We shall see later, however, when we come to consider the work of Marx, that the two need not be regarded as alternatives.

I am grateful to the two anonymous readers who commented valuably on an earlier draft of this book, not least to the brutal suggestion by one of them that I cut the first forty pages. In my view, the work has profited greatly from this amputation. Rachael Lonsdale, my editor at Yale University Press, has now steered half a dozen books of mine through the press with a preternaturally keen eye for loose phrasing and structural incoherence. She is the best of editors, and I owe her a deep debt of gratitude.

T.E.

CHAPTER ONE

Materialisms

MATERIALISM COMES IN various shapes and sizes. There are hard-nosed versions of it as well as soft-bellied ones. Given the daunting size of the subject, however, not to speak of my own intellectual limitations, only some of these currents of materialist thought will be the concern of this book. My interest is not in certain highly technical questions of monism, dualism, eliminativism or the mind–body problem in general, but in forms of materialism that are in some broad sense social or political, and about which the neuroscientists have had for the most part nothing very exciting to say.

If you are the kind of materialist who holds that material conditions set the pace in human affairs, you may seek to change these conditions in the hope that you may thereby alter the way people think and act. If your materialism is of a deterministic kind, one which regards men and women as wholly conditioned by their environments, this project may well seem a promising one. The problem is that if individuals are mere functions of their surroundings, then this must also apply to you, in which case how can you act to transform that context if you yourself are a product of it? Despite such troubling queries, materialism has been traditionally (though not exclusively) allied with political radicalism. Empiricist materialists such as the eighteenth-century English thinkers David Hartley and Joseph Priestley held that the mind was made up of sense-impressions; that sense-impressions stemmed from one's environment; and that if this environment could be so refashioned as to generate the 'right' kinds of sense data, human behaviour could be dramatically changed for the better.[1] Politically speaking, this was not an unambiguously progressive project. As Marx would later point out, the alteration in question was generally in the service of the rulers' own needs and interests. He was not slow to detect the politics implicit in this theory of knowledge.

There is a link between radicalism and materialism in some of the left-wing thought of the English Civil War, as there is in the work of Baruch Spinoza and the *philosophes* of the French Enlightenment. It is a legacy that descends to Marx and Engels, and which crops up in our own time in the work of such dissident theorists as Gilles Deleuze. (Darwin, Nietzsche and Freud are also radical materialists, but not thinkers of the far left.) Though the word 'materialism' was coined in the eighteenth century, the doctrine itself is an ancient one,[2] and one of its earliest exponents, the Greek philosopher Epicurus, was the subject of Marx's doctoral thesis. Marx admired Epicurus's passion for justice and liberty, his distaste for the accumulation of wealth, his enlightened attitude to women and the seriousness with which he took the sensuous nature of humanity, all of which he saw as bound up with his philosophical views. Materialism for Epicurus, as for the Enlightenment, meant among other things freedom from priestcraft and superstition.

For Isaac Newton and his colleagues, matter was brute, inert stuff ('stupid', Newton called it) and as such had to be set in motion by the external power of the divine will. The point has a bearing on the human body. Those who look upon the body rather as they regard a corpse are likely to feel the need to add some ghostly entity to it if it is to be galvanised into action. Gross and sluggish as it is, it is hardly likely to activate itself. In this sense, disembodied minds and souls are among other things an attempt to compensate for the crudities of mechanical materialism. If one took a less mechanistic view of matter, they might well prove superfluous. If spirit and Nature are distinct domains, then the former is free to exert its sway over the latter. In the Newtonian view, spiritual forces rule Nature from above rather as monarchs and despots govern their states.

For the radical lineage stemming from Spinoza, by contrast, there is no call for such august authorities. Matter itself is alive, and not only alive but self-determining, rather like the populace of a democratic state. It is unnecessary to posit a sovereign power that sets it in motion. Besides, to repudiate a realm of spirits is to take the material world with unswerving seriousness, along with the material well-being of the men and women in it. It admits of no ethereal distractions from the business of setting poverty and injustice to rights. It also allows one to reject all clerical authority, since if spirit is everywhere one looks then the priesthood can have no monopoly on it. It is thus that one can speak of a politics of matter.

To be a materialist in this sense is to invest human beings with a degree of dignity by seeing them as part of a material world which is identical with the Almighty. Such, at least, was the view of the pantheistic Spinoza. Materialism and humanism are thus natural bedfellows. By the same token, however, you could take a smack at those more conservative humanists for whom there was an unbridgeable gulf between humanity and the rest of Nature. Such philosophical lordliness could be undercut by pointing to the humdrum status of humanity, humbly at one with the material world and its fellow animals. Humanity is not Lord of Creation but part of its communality, our flesh and sinews woven of the same stuff as the forces that stir the waves and ripen the cornfields. As Friedrich Engels remarks in *The Dialectics of Nature*:

we by no means rule over nature like a conqueror over a foreign people, like someone standing outside nature – but we, with flesh, blood and brain, belong to nature, and exist in its midst, and . . . all our mastery of it consists in the fact that we have the advantage over other beings of being able to know and correctly apply its laws.[3]

Not long before, Darwin had laid bare our lowly origins, displacing a humanity that would have preferred some more noble provenance for itself into an unglamorous mesh of material processes.

There is, then, an ethical dimension to materialism as well as a political one. In the face of a hubristic humanism, it insists on our solidarity with the commonplace stuff of the world, thus cultivating the virtue of humility. Dismayed by the fantasy that human beings are wholly self-determining, it recalls us to our dependence on our surroundings and on each other. 'The original helplessness of human beings,' writes Sigmund Freud, 'is . . . the primal source of all moral motives.'[4] What makes us moral beings is not our autonomy but our vulnerability, not our self-closure but our open-endedness. True to this materialist spirit, the Marxist philosopher Sebastiano Timpanaro writes of how

the results of scientific research teach us that man occupies a marginal position in the universe; that for a very long time life did not exist on earth, and that its origin depended on very special conditions; that human thought is conditioned by determinate anatomical and physiological structures, and is clouded or impeded by determinate pathological alterations of these . . . [5]

Materialism of this kind fosters not nihilism but realism. As in the art of tragedy, our achievements, if they are to be well founded, must involve acknowledging our frailty and finitude. There are other moral benefits, too. Aware of the intractability of matter, materialist thought promotes a respect for the otherness and integrity of the world, in contrast to the postmodern narcissism that sees nothing but reflections of human culture wherever it looks. Materialism is equally sceptical of the postmodern prejudice for which reality is clay in our hands, to be stretched, hacked, pummelled and remoulded by the imperious will. It is a late-capitalist version of the old Gnostic aversion to matter.

Marxists like Timpanaro are also exponents of so-called historical materialism, which we shall have more to say about later.[6] Some of them (though a dwindling band these days) are also advocates of dialectical materialism, sometimes known more simply as Marxist philosophy.[7] Historical materialism, as the term suggests, is a theory of history, whereas dialectical materialism, the founding work of which is Engels' *Dialectics of Nature*, is a vastly more ambitious vision of reality. Its

6

theoretical horizon is nothing less than the cosmos itself, which is doubtless one reason why it is out of favour in these pragmatic times. From ants to asteroids, the world is a dynamic complex of interlocking forces in which all phenomena are interrelated, nothing stays still, quantity converts into quality, no absolute standpoints are available, everything is perpetually on the point of turning into its opposite and reality evolves through the unity of conflicting powers. Those who deny this doctrine stand accused of being metaphysicians, falsely assuming that phenomena are stable, autonomous and discrete, that there are no contradictions in reality and that everything is itself and not some other thing.

It is not clear what to make of the claim that everything is related to everything else. There seems little in common between the Pentagon and a sudden upsurge of sexual jealousy, other than the fact that neither can ride a bicycle. Some of the laws that dialectical materialism finds at work in the world cut across the distinction between Nature and culture, a case which sails embarrassingly close to the bourgeois positivism Marxism rejects. As a Marxist worker of my acquaintance triumphantly put it: 'Kettles boil, dogs' tails wag and classes struggle.' There are plenty of Marxists, however, for whom dialectical materialism is either a disguised form of idealism or philosophical nonsense.[8] The latter was the opinion of a group of so-called analytic Marxists some years ago who were in the habit of sporting T-shirts bearing the slogan 'Marxisme sans la merde de taureau', or 'Marxism without the bullshit'.

It is worth noting that historical materialists need not be atheists, though many of them seem curiously ignorant of the fact. Though most of them reject religious belief, they generally fail to recognise that there is no logical connection between the two cases. Historical materialism is not an ontological affair. It does not assert that everything is made out of matter, and that God is therefore an absurdity. Nor is it a Theory of Everything, as dialectical materialism aspires to be. It has nothing of pressing importance to say about the optic nerve or how to rustle up the fluffiest soufflé. It is a far more modest proposal – one which views class struggle, along with a conflict between the forces and relations of production, as the dynamic of epochal historical change. It also regards the material activities of men and women as lying at the source of their social existence, a view which is not confined to Marxism. There is no reason why a religious Jew like Walter Benjamin or a devotee of Christian liberation theology should not sign on for this way of seeing. There have also been Islamic Marxists. In theory, you could look forward to the inevitable triumph of the proletariat while spending several hours a day prostrate before a statue of the Virgin Mary. It would be less easy to hold that matter is all there is and believe in the Archangel Gabriel.

Dialectical materialism, so some have argued, belongs to a current of vitalist materialism which passes from Democritus and Epicurus to Spinoza, Schelling, Nietzsche, Henri Bergson, Ernst Bloch, Gilles Deleuze and a range of other thinkers. One benefit of this creed is that it allows you to make room for spirit without going disreputably dualist, since spirit, in the form of life or energy, is built into matter itself. It has also, however, been rebuked as a form of irrationalism. Reality on this view is volatile, mercurial and constantly mutating, and the mind, which tends to carve up the world according to certain rather arthritic categories, finds it hard to keep abreast of this constant flux. Consciousness is too maladroit and cumbersome a faculty to cope with the intricacies of Nature. Whereas the mind used to outrun the inertia of matter, matter is now quicksilver stuff that outstrips mind.

There are strains of vitalism that tend to idealise and etherealise matter. As such, they run the risk of taking the pain out of it, turning their gaze from its recalcitrant bulk.[9] Matter on this benign view is no longer what hurts – what spikes our projects and baffles our aims – but instead assumes all the fineness and malleability of spirit. It is a strangely immaterial brand of materialism. As Slavoj Žižek remarks, the so-called New Materialism which promotes this view

is materialist in the sense in which Tolkien's Middle-earth is materialist: as an enchanted world full of magic forces, good and evil spirits, etc., but strangely *without gods* – there are no transcendent divine entities in Tolkien's universe, all magic is immanent to matter, as a spiritual power that dwells in our terrestrial world.[10]

Like Tolkien's, it is essentially a pagan vision. As the editors of a volume entitled *New Materialisms* put it, 'materiality is always something more than "mere" matter: an excess, force, vitality, relationality, or difference that renders matter active, self-creating, productive, unpredictable'.[11]

Another piece in the same volume describes matter as 'a vital principle that inhabits us and our inventions',[12] which lends it pseudo-metaphysical status. Yet another contributor writes that 'the deconstructive understanding of materiality indicates a force that is impossible, something not yet and no longer of the order of presence and the possible'.[13] With the Derridean buzzword 'impossible', materialism would now seem to be moving rapidly in the direction of the apophatic or ineffable. Rey Chow calls for 'a revamped materialism defined primarily as signification and subject-in-process',[14] which is rather like calling for a revamped idea of a rhino defined primarily as a rabbit. Why should 'signification and subject-in-process' be thought the prime example of materialism?

Matter, in short, must be rescued from the humiliation of being matter. Instead, it must be regarded as a sort of materiality without substance, as fluid and protean as the post-structuralist notion of textuality. Like textuality, the stuff is infinite, indeterminate, unpredictable, non-stratified, diffuse, free-floating, heterogeneous and untotalisable. Eric Santner aptly describes the case as 'a sort of multiculturalism at the cellular level'.[15] It is obvious enough from *New Materialisms* that the brand of materialism it advocates is really a species of post-structuralism in wolf's clothing. Where thinkers like Jacques Derrida say 'text', new materialists say 'matter'. Otherwise, not much has changed.

Like many an apparent innovation, then, the New Materialism is by no means as new as it seems. It shares post-structuralism's suspicion of humanism – of the belief that human beings occupy a privileged place in the world – and seeks to discredit this view with a vision of material forces that flow indifferently across both human and natural spheres. But you cannot play down what is peculiar to humanity simply by animating everything around it. Matter may be alive, but it is not alive in the sense that human beings are. It cannot despair, embezzle, murder or get married. The moon may be in some sense a living being, but it cannot prefer Schoenberg to Stravinsky. Particles of matter do not move within a world of meaning, as people do. Humans can have history, but poppies and bagpipes cannot. Matter may be self-activating, but this is not the same as achieving one's ends. Matter has no ends to achieve.

If vitalism rejects a view of matter as brute, insensate stuff, it is partly because it would seem to leave room for disembodied spirits. If you reduce human bodies to the status of coffee tables, you might feel the need to tack an impalpable soul onto them to make sense of a lot of what they get up to. Mechanical materialism can thus easily capsize into its opposite. Against its own intentions, it may clear the way to assigning humanity a unique spiritual status. Vitalism is right to reject the false dichotomy between dumb matter and immortal spirit, but it does so by claiming that all matter is alive, which simply elevates coffee tables to the level of humans. The truth is that men and women are neither set apart from the material world (as for idealist humanism), or mere pieces of matter (as for mechanical materialism). They are indeed pieces of matter, but pieces of matter of a peculiar kind. Or, as Marx puts it: human beings are part of Nature, which is to think of the two as inseparable; but we can also speak of them as being 'linked', which is to point up their difference.[16] Some vitalist materialists fear that to highlight the difference between humans and the rest of Nature is to establish an invidious hierarchy. But men and women are indeed in some ways more creative than hedgehogs. They are also unspeakably more destructive, and for much the same reasons. Those who deny the former are at risk of ignoring the latter.

Human beings are outcrops of the material world, but that is not to say that they are no different from toadstools.

They differ from them not because they are spiritual while toadstools are material, but because they are instances of that peculiar form of materiality known as being an animal. They also have a peculiar status within the animal kingdom, which is by no means to say an unambiguously 'higher' one. The New Materialism, by contrast, is too quick to see talk of the special nature of humanity only as arrogance or idealism. It is a postmodern brand of materialism. Alarmed by the prospect of privilege – of a disabling division between human creatures and the rest of Nature – it risks levelling such distinctions in a spirit of cosmic egalitarianism, while pluralising matter itself. In doing so, it ends up with the kind of contemplative vision of the world that (as we shall see later) Marx criticises in Feuerbach. You do not escape such a standpoint by seeing everything as vital and dynamic rather than mechanical and inert.

If reductive materialism finds it hard to make room for the human subject, not least for the subject as agent, so too does this 'new' version of the doctrine. Whereas mechanical materialism suspects that human agency is an illusion, vitalist materialism is out to decentre the all-sovereign subject into the mesh of material forces that constitute it. In drawing attention to those forces, however, it sometimes fails to recognise that one can be an autonomous agent without being magically free of determinations. Autonomy is rather a question of relating to such determinations in a peculiar way. To be self-determining does not mean ceasing to be dependent on the world around us. In fact, it is only through dependence (on those who nurture us, for example) that we can achieve a degree of independence in the first place. The autonomous subject set up by most postmodern thought is a straw man. To be free of all determinations would not be freedom at all. How could one be free to score a goal for Real Madrid if one's legs did not operate in a certain anatomically determined, reliably predictable way?

In *New Materialisms*, as in most forms of vitalism, terms like 'life' and 'energy' hover ambiguously between the descriptive and the normative. In designating certain dynamic forces, the authors also tend to invest them with value, despite the fact that by no means all manifestations of life, force and energy are to be commended. Not all dynamism is to be admired, as the career of Donald Trump might testify. A view of matter as mutable, multiple and diffuse can also bring with it a distaste for 'constraining' social institutions and political organisations. It is thus possible to move from New Materialism to anti-Marxism in a few excessively rapid steps.

Some of the chief vices of vitalism can be found in the work of Gilles Deleuze, a full-blooded metaphysician for whom Being consists in an immanent creativity which is both infinite and absolute, and of which the highest expression is pure thought.[17] In the Gnostic universe of Deleuze's *The Logic of Sense, Anti-Oedipus* and *Difference and Repetition*, subjects, bodies, organs, agents, discourses, histories and institutions – in fact, actuality as such – threaten to obstruct this virtual, unfathomable force, rather as the body was traditionally thought to incarcerate the soul. For the most part, Deleuze can see constraint only as negative, a view that faithfully reflects the marketplace ideology he otherwise finds objectionable. History, ethics, law, property, territory, signification, work, family, subjectivity, everyday sexuality and mass political organisation are by and large normalising, castrating, regularising, colonising powers, as they are, by and large, for Deleuze's admirer Michel Foucault. One must look askance at unity, abstraction, mediation, signification, relationality, interiority, interpretation, representation, intentionality and reconciliation. From the viewpoint of an alienated intelligentsia, there is little that is constructive to be discovered in everyday social existence. Instead, with a handful of qualifying clauses, we are offered a banal antithesis between the vital, creative, desirous and dynamic (to be unequivocally endorsed) and the oppressive realm of stable material forms (to be implicitly demonised). Deleuze's cosmic vitalism is virulently anti-materialist. 'Life' is an etherealising force, blankly indifferent to corporeal human beings, whose highest attainment is to divest themselves of their creatureliness so as to become the pliant medium of this implacable power. The chief question is how we can be rid of ourselves. Some of those who applaud aspects of Deleuze's case reject it out of hand when they stumble upon it in different guise in the writing of D.H. Lawrence.

What we are offered, then, is a Romantic-libertarian philosophy of unbridled affirmation and incessant innovation, as though the creative and innovative were unambiguously on the side of the angels. It is a universe without lack or flaw, indifferent to breakdown and tragedy. Being is univocal, which means that all things are faces of God or facets of the life force. Human beings are accordingly raised to quasi-divine status; but by the same token God loses his transcendence and merges with material reality, as he does for Deleuze's great mentor, Spinoza. In what Heidegger regards as the characteristic error of metaphysics, Being is modelled on beings, so that God becomes in idolatrous style an all-powerful Super-Object. Besides, if we are all part of an immanent Deity, then we can have access to absolute reality simply by knowing ourselves, since it is this Absolute which thinks and feels in us. I can know the truth simply by consulting my own intuitions.

Whatever else the political implications of such a case may be, they are certainly not on the side of radicalism, although the case advanced in *New Materialisms* presents itself as precisely that. Yet it is not hard to see how well it consorts with the nature of post-industrial capitalism – with a world in which labour and capital are dematerialised into signs, flows and codes; social phenomena are mobile, plural and ceaselessly mutable; and images, simulacra and virtualities hold sway over anything as grossly simplistic as material objects. In this infinitely plastic environment, the sheer intractability of matter presents something of a scandal. A materialistic society harbours no great affection for the material, since it can always muster a degree of resistance to its ends. Not all vitalist materialism has been notable for its progressive politics. Mormonism, not generally considered the most socially enlightened of creeds, is one such example. For its founder, Joseph Smith, spirit is simply a finer, purer variety of matter – gentrified matter, so to speak. Materiality is eminently acceptable as long as it is hard to distinguish from spirit. The New Materialism emerged in part to replace a currently unfashionable historical materialism. Yet whole currents of it would seem to have no particular concern, as historical materialism does, with the destiny of men and women in an exploitative world.

* * *

What other varieties of materialism are on offer? There is cultural materialism, the brainchild of the British cultural critic Raymond Williams, which investigates works of art in their material contexts.[18] For all its undoubted insights, it is not easy to see how this is much more than a politicised version of the traditional sociology of art, which also enquires into such questions as audiences, readerships, the social institutions of culture and the like. There is also semantic materialism, a style of thought popular in the high-theoretical 1970s but not greatly in vogue nowadays. It argues that signifiers are material (marks, sounds and so on); that signifieds or meanings are the product of an interplay of signifiers; and that meaning accordingly has a material foundation. Ludwig Wittgenstein, as we shall see later, regards meaning as a question of how material signs function within a practical form of life. If the life of a sign lies in its use, and its use is a material matter, then it is not as though its sense lurks somewhere behind it, as the soul for a Cartesian dualist lies concealed within the body. We are tempted to imagine, Wittgenstein notes in *The Blue and Brown Books*, that there is an 'inorganic' or material part to the handling of signs, and then an organic or spiritual aspect which is meaning and understanding.[19] This, however, is in his view a false dichotomy. Meaning is a matter of what we get up to with signs, of how we deploy them for specific ends in the public world. It is no more invisible than the act of wielding a can-opener. Understanding is the mastery of a technique, and as such a form of practice.[20]

Like many apparently modern ideas, semantic materialism has its source in antiquity. It is also to be found in the writings of Marx, who observes that 'the element of thought itself, the element of the vital expression of thought – *language* – is sensuous nature'.[21] It is matter (marks, sounds, gestures) that is constitutive of meaning. Marx speaks in *The German Ideology* of language as dismantling the distinction between matter and spirit, which as we shall see later is also true of the body. In a sardonic smack at the philosophical idealists, he notes with mock regret how 'from the start the "spirit" is afflicted with the curse of being "burdened" with matter, which here makes its appearance in the form of agitated layers of air, sounds, in short, of language'.[22] 'Afflicted', 'curse', 'burdened': Marx is writing here in satirical Swiftian vein, affecting to see the purity of human meaning as contaminated by its lowly material medium. Can such lofty conceptions as the Supreme Being or the Platonic Forms really come to us in the form of agitated layers of air? Are they not exalted enough to exist independently of sound or script? By what mystery can humble black marks on a white page designate human notions, interests and desires?

'Language is as old as consciousness', Marx continues. 'Language *is* practical consciousness that exists also for other men, and for that reason alone it really exists for me personally as well; language, like consciousness, only arises from the need, the necessity, of intercourse with other men.'[23] If Wittgenstein, as we shall see, insists on the public nature of language, as well as on its involvement with the rest of our material existence, Marx anticipates his insights, in however cursory a form. If language is practical consciousness, and if the signs that make it up are material, then we can speak at a stretch of the materiality of consciousness. It is just that what the phrase means for Marx is not for the most part what it means for contemporary neuroscience.

Language is the work of no single individual, so that this badge of our humanity has a curiously anonymous air to it. It is less a personal possession than a medium into which we are born. For the most part, the finest of poets can give voice to their most intimate feelings only by drawing upon terms that innumerable men and women have employed countless times before. There are, of course, such things as neologisms, but these make sense only in terms of already established meanings. So we are faced with the materialist paradox that the human is born of the non-human. Of course language is in some sense a human invention. But it bears in upon us with a certain implacable force. It is as much a fatality as an arena of creativity. And this is true of more than language. We are also the product of history, heredity, systems of kinship, social institutions and unconscious processes. These are not for the most part things we choose. They, too, weigh in upon us like impersonal powers, even though (with the exception of biology) they are at root human creations. The human subject is thus always to some degree a stranger to itself, constituted by powers it is incapable of fully appropriating; and that this is so is part of the materialist case. It is idealism that begins with the subject as though it were self-born, and thus fails to start far back enough.

Samantha Frost writes illuminatingly of how the greatest of English political philosophers, Thomas Hobbes, reveals a quasi-Nietzschean sense of the unfathomable complexity which goes into our making. He is alert to the subtle interweaving of the powers that constitute us – of the role of custom, habit, fortune, bodily constitution, contingent experiences and so on in the manufacture of so-called autonomous human agents.[24] That we are a product of so many forces is not to claim with the eliminativists that human agency is a self-serving myth. It is rather to insist that what self-determination we can achieve exists within the context of a deeper dependency. The fact that our flesh is derived from the flesh of others is one palpable mark of this. Nothing can spring from its own loins and still be human. The most visible sign of our agency-cum-dependency is the body, which is the source of our activity yet which is also mortal, fragile and fearfully susceptible to pain. If the body is the medium of agency, it is also a cause of affliction. It is what renders us vulnerable as well as productive. It is because we are lumps of flesh of a certain kind that we are capable of being historical agents; but to be a body also means to be exposed and unprotected, subject to numerous uncontrollable influences, incapable of complete self-mastery. As Joeri Schrijvers comments, 'being-in-the-world as a body entails both facticity and freedom, both spontaneous givenness and active constitution'.[25] We cannot decide not to breathe or bleed, since like the unconscious (and somatic processes are themselves unconscious), the body imposes its own rigorously anonymous logic upon our lives.

It is in this spirit that Sebastiano Timpanaro reminds us that 'we cannot deny or evade the element of passivity in experience: the external situation which we do not create but which imposes itself on us'.[26] To see human beings primarily as agents is not to succumb to some cult of frenetic activism. Because we are rational *animals*, we are subject to various forms of hardship and exploitation. 'As a natural, corporeal, sensuous, objective being,' writes Marx, '[the human individual] is a suffering, conditioned and limited being.'[27] Because we are *rational* animals, and thus peculiarly resourceful, some (though not all) of these ills can be repaired. Pain is a reminder of the facticity of the flesh, its stubborn resistance to spirit. The body is a chunk of matter we never get to choose, and which we can never fully appropriate. If it is our expressive medium, it also retains its own density and part-autonomy. For Jean-Luc Nancy, it represents that which thought can never fully penetrate, even if it is the ground and origin of our thinking.[28]

There is a sense, then, in which the very material basis of subjectivity threatens to undermine it. As fleshly creatures, we bear about with us something of the dense, refractory nature of matter, only now as close to us as breathing. In Jacques Lacan's useful neologism, the body is 'extimate'. Like death, it is both a fate wished upon us and intimately one's own. If it is a mode of individuation, it is also a common condition. What makes us inimitably ourselves is stuff we share with countless billions of others. To individuate oneself, as Marx points out, is a capacity that belongs to our species-being in general. That we can become unique persons is an aspect of our shared animality.

Given its impersonality, the body can feel strangely extraneous to the self, so that dualism is in a sense an understandable mistake. Dualists are not wrong to see human beings as self-divided; they simply misidentify the nature of this fissure. It is not that we are split between the lumpish body and an ethereal entity called the soul. Even when we objectify our own bodies, or feel them as an encumbrance on the spirit, the self that has such experiences is an embodied phenomenon. To feel one's flesh as alien and external is actually part of one's 'soul', in the sense of one's significant life as an organism. We are at odds with ourselves not because body and soul are mutually at odds, but because of the temporal, creative, open-ended animals that we are. We shall see later that to speak of the soul is to denote the kind of body that is capable of signifying; and because there is no end to signification, we are unfinished creatures perpetually in process and out ahead of ourselves. To call ourselves historical beings is to say that we are constitutively capable of self-transcendence, becoming at one with ourselves only in death. Besides, as creatures of desire, we are continually split between what we possess and what we aspire to, as well as between what we consciously imagine we desire and what we unconsciously do. It is in these and other senses that we are split subjects, not because we are an awkward amalgam of brute matter and pure mind. The soul has sometimes been seen as the essence of the body, its principle of unity; but it is actually a way of describing how we are never quite identical with ourselves.

Every time we act, we dismantle the distinction between matter and spirit, interweaving meaning and materiality; but it is only in certain special contexts (dancing, making love, playing world-class tennis) that the body seems luminously transparent to the mind. On these rare occasions, the material and phenomenological bodies seem to converge.[29] For some aesthetic theory, this convergence is consummated above all in the work of art. What strikes us as special about the aesthetic artefact is that every material particle of it seems informed by an integral meaning, and so reveals a harmony between sense as meaning and sense as substance. This, as it happens, is also true of the Christian doctrine of the risen human body. The risen or transfigured body transcends the tension between having a body and being one – between the body as given and the body as expressive. As with a piece of poetry, its material stuff is at one with its meaning.

When St Paul writes disparagingly of the flesh, he is speaking not of our physical nature but of a specific way of life, one in which the body and its desires spin out of control and become monstrously insubordinate. His name for this mode of existence is sin. The body (*soma*) is in Paul's Hebraic view blessed because it is God's creation, while the flesh (*sarx*) is his metaphor for the way it can grow perverse and pathological. When it comes to the flesh, we are in the realm of neurotic compulsions and pathological repetitions, of desires that become rigid and despotic. In this sense, Paul might be said to foreshadow some of the insights of Sigmund Freud. As a somatic materialist, Freud sees the busy traffic between the body of the infant and those of its carers as lying at the source of the human spirit, but also at the root of its sickness. It is from this intimate commerce that the child's gratitude to those who nurture it first arises, a sentiment that in Freud's judgement is the foundation of morality. It is here, too, however, that desire first germinates and the unconscious is opened up; and these forces will warp the psyche from within, bending our projects and perceptions out of true. For Freud, then, the life of the unconscious springs from the kind of material animals that we are. As Alfred Schmidt remarks, 'the understanding of man as a needy, sensuous, physiological being is . . . the precondition of any theory of subjectivity'.[30] Part of that subjectivity concerns that within us which outstrips the conscious mind. The fantasia of the unconscious springs from the most mundane of situations – the infant's need for the constant ministrations of its carers, without which it will die. It is the upshot of material necessity.

While the baby is still in this state, the 'Fall' into language and desire has not yet happened. Instead, there is a set of tacit somatic understandings between the child and its caregivers on which language will eventually build. As human communication grows more elaborate, however, it becomes thicker in one sense but thinner in another – richer and more complex, yet also perilously abstract, and thus capable of being cut free from the sensuous control of the flesh. We can no longer rely upon instinct and bodily reflex, but are thrown back instead on the more precarious resources of reason. Language, so to speak, no longer has the backing of the body, as it does with Clym Yeobright and his mother in Thomas Hardy's novel *The Return of the Native*, whose 'discourses were as if carried on between the right and the left hands of the same body'. Body and language can thus come to be at odds with each other; and this, too, can be misinterpreted as a war between body and soul.

Ludwig Wittgenstein was an admirer of Freud, a fellow Viennese whose works were well known to his family. Indeed, few families were more sorely in need of Freud's ministrations than this psychically disabled bunch, though only Ludwig's sister Margarethe was actually analysed by him.[31] Wittgenstein's attitude to infants, for example, is much closer to Freud's than it is to the conventional wisdom of suburban England. 'Anyone who listens to a child's crying with understanding,' he writes, 'will know that psychic forces, terrible forces, sleep within it, different from anything commonly assumed. Profound rage and pain and lust for destruction.'[32] If infants do not do us harm, as St Augustine dryly remarks in his *Confessions*, it is for lack of strength, not lack of will. Wittgenstein and his sister both submitted themselves to hypnosis, and having put up some robust resistance to the process fell into a deep trance as soon as the session was over. Even on the hypnotist's couch, Wittgenstein had a lordly way with convention. There is no reason to think that his and Freud's outlooks are mutually incompatible.[33] Wittgenstein's insistence on the public accessibility of our 'inner' states does not rule out the fact that they may be ambiguous and elusive. And one reason for this may well be the stratagems of the unconscious. Neither thinker saw men and women as transparent to themselves. For Wittgenstein, we can easily be deceived about what we are feeling; for Freud, we live in a permanent state of self-opacity known as the unconscious. The human subject emerges from a failure to be identical with itself.

* * *

We may turn now to so-called speculative materialism, a theory associated with the French philosopher Quentin Meillassoux.[34] Like Timpanaro, Meillassoux is out to dislodge the human subject from the privileged status with which an idealist humanism invests it. He, too, draws attention to the vast stretches of cosmic time (what he calls 'ancestrality') before humanity emerged on earth. For idealism, the world can be known only from the standpoint of a specific subject (what Meillassoux dubs 'correlationism'), but in his view there is more to our cognitive powers than this. We can also know that this correlation between subject and object is contingent. There is no necessity for it, or indeed for anything else. In a material world, nothing need be the case, and everything could have been entirely otherwise. Nothing could be further from the thought of a determinist like Spinoza, who argues in his *Ethics* that 'in the universe there exists nothing contingent, but all things are determined by the necessity of the divine nature to exist and operate in a certain way'.[35]

Contingency, to be sure, does not mean chaos. It is not that one's children might wake up one morning speaking fluent Farsi, a language of which they were ignorant when they went to bed. There is indeed law and logic, but the fact that there is is itself non-necessary. Absolute knowledge is not a question of searching out the essences of things, but of knowing that they have no essences. Even flux is contingent. There might always have been fixity instead. In *The Divine Inexistence*,[36] Meillassoux says that such contingent status is true even of God. There is in fact no God, but there always could be. He might always pop into existence next Wednesday, perhaps sometime between lunch and high tea. What is logically possible is also actually possible. We may not know whether a certain logical proposition is true of the world, but we know that it always could be. Since Meillassoux regards this contingency as the fundamental truth of reality, he is that rare kind of materialist for whom it is possible to know the Absolute.

Speculative materialism insists on the fragility of humankind when silhouetted against the backdrop of cosmic time and space. Anthropomorphism is a form of stupidity. Yet Meillassoux is also an ardent champion of infinitude, like his philosophical mentor Alain Badiou. In a material world, nothing is in principle out of bounds to reason. To set limits to reason in the manner of Immanuel Kant is to allow for the possibility of transcendence – for phenomena that lie beyond the reach of human rationality. And this is to let in a good deal of vacuous spirituality, as well as a tidal wave of religious fanaticism. For a stout Gallic rationalist like Meillassoux, however, there can be no terrain on which the writ of reason does not run. Thought is in principle infinite. It knows no natural closure. The existence of God would place limits on our understanding, whereas his absence means that our cognitive enquiries are potentially boundless.

Ironically, it is because there is no God that we can have access to the Absolute – which is to say, to a knowledge of the utter contingency of things. If a deity did exist, then the world would be governed by divine necessity; one, perhaps, whose operations were known to God alone; and contingency would cease to be the ultimate truth of it. In this sense, Meillassoux is a good old-fashioned medieval nominalist who holds that God must be banished from the world if its freedom is to be preserved, in contrast to the more orthodox view that God is himself the source of that freedom. Miracles, he mischievously suggests, testify to the non-existence of the Almighty, since they point to a lack of cosmic design.

As long as we can claim that there is a necessary reason why things are as they are, we can also suppose that there is a necessary reason for the world as a whole, which for Meillassoux would mean capitulating to theism. If something has such a reason, so some have argued, then that reason must itself have a reason; and if we are to avoid an infinite regress of such reasons we must posit an end point to this chain of iron necessities known as God, who is his own *raison d'être*. Meillassoux is out to reject this way of seeing, which he perhaps mistakenly takes to be one of Thomas Aquinas's arguments for the existence of God. Instead, it is vital that we refuse to surrender to theism, not least because contingency in Meillassoux's view lies at the foundation of ethics. Because the world is not governed by divine laws, it is provisional, open-ended and thus hospitable to hope. Atheism, not theism, is the foundation of the good life.

Speculative materialism, then, holds that there is no reason for the cosmos, and that to imagine otherwise is to fall prey to theism. For orthodox Christian theology, however, it is exactly the non-necessity of the world which points to God. The doctrine of Creation holds among other things that the universe is purely contingent. God made it not out of necessity, since there is nothing that he must necessarily do, but out of love. The world on this view is purely gratuitous, perpetually overshadowed by the possibility of its own non-existence; and it is this gratuitousness – what the novelist Milan Kundera calls 'the unbearable lightness of being' – that alludes to its Creator, rather than any specific item of the cosmos itself. The universe is gift rather than fatality. To resort to a technical theological term, God made it just for the hell of it, out of his own eternal self-delight, rather as an artist produces a painting. It is he who is the supreme guarantor of the contingency of things. The fact that there is anything at all, given that there might just as well have been nothing, is on account of him. Meillassoux thus fails to understand the theology he rejects. But this is nothing new. Most atheists set up theological straw men, which they then proceed to bowl triumphantly over.

It is structuralism, of all things, that can throw some light on the idea of Creation. For this style of thought, every item of the world appears against the background of its potential absence – which is to say that all such items are arbitrary and mutually exchangeable. It is only the locations they occupy within an overall structure that remain constant. It doesn't matter which colour you use for 'Go' on your traffic lights as long as it isn't the colour you use for 'Stop'. When one entity is substituted for another, its contingency is thrown into relief;

and this, in turn, makes newly perceptible the places these entities occupy, as that which survives their coming and going. It is as though the places themselves can appear only in negative fashion, as we cease to identify something with the space it fills and instead, in the transition between one temporary occupant and another, gain a glimpse of the location itself.

In a similar way, it is the contingency of the world that reveals its Creator. God is the backdrop that becomes visible only against the constant emerging and passing away of things. As the poet Rilke puts it, he is the one who holds all this endless falling in his hands. Yet it is not exactly that contingency leads us in Platonic style to posit something necessary and eternal lying beyond it. It is rather that any particular non-necessary fact points to the non-necessity of the world as a whole. It suggests that there might just as well have been nothing as something; and for the theologian, the reason why this is not so is God, who loved the universe into being in a purely gratuitous act. Nothingness in the sense of the non-being with which the world is shot through (namely, the fact that it has no need to exist) points to nothingness in the sense of the unfathomable abyss which is the Deity. It is this that the doctrine of Creation is trying to capture. It has nothing to do with how the world got started. You could still hold this view while believing with Aristotle that the world never had an origin at all.

* * *

Materialism is a remarkably capacious concept. It stretches all the way from the mind–body problem to the question of whether the state exists primarily to defend private property. It can mean a denial of God, a belief that the Great Wall of China and Clint Eastwood's ankles are secretly interrelated, or an insistence that the Golden Gate Bridge continues to exist when nobody is looking at it. Yet it also has an everyday meaning, one that is not in the least philosophical. Materialism for most people means an excessive regard for material goods. 'By the word materialism,' writes Friedrich Engels, 'the philistine understands gluttony, drunkenness, lust of the eye, lust of the flesh, arrogance, cupidity, avarice, covetousness, profit-hunting and stock-exchange swindling – in short, all the filthy vices in which he himself indulges in private.'[37] To call Madonna materialistic is not to say that she holds that spirit is simply matter in motion, or that classes struggle in much the same way that dogs' tails wag. It is, however, to cast light on her interest in an off-the-peg version of Kabbalah, just as it casts light on John Travolta's sinister enthusiasm for Scientology. People who have a surplus of material goods are likely to resort to bogus forms of spirituality as a much-needed refuge from them. A gullible belief in wood nymphs, magic crystals, Theosophy or alien spacecraft is simply the flipside of their worldliness. It is no wonder that Tarot, packaged occultism and ready-to-serve transcendence should be so fashionable in the Hollywood hills.

The spiritual in this view is not a specific mode of materiality – a question of feeding the hungry, welcoming the stranger, falling in love, celebrating friendship, speaking up for justice and so on – but a flight from such drearily mundane matters. It offers you a welcome respite from a glut of minders, agents, hair stylists and heated swimming pools. It represents the bad faith of the fabulously rich. There were a good many British colonialists in India who found in Indian spirituality a temporary escape from the tiresome necessity of knocking the natives about. It is said that Heinrich Himmler always carried a copy of the *Bhagavad Gita* with him. If (in a vulgarised version of Hinduism) the world is illusion, then everything is permissible.

There is, finally, a broad use of the word 'materialism' to mean a delicate responsiveness to material process. We may speak of this Keatsian vigilance to the flow and texture of material things as the materialist imagination, a phrase which in some other contexts might seem an oxymoron. It is a sense of the term superbly illustrated on almost every page of Marilynne Robinson's novel *Housekeeping*.

So far, we have surveyed an assortment of materialisms, some of which we will examine further. One type that will concern us most, however, is neither cultural nor semantic, vitalist nor speculative, mechanical nor dialectical. Nor is it a question of stashing away a few extra Range Rovers in the garage. It bears a relation to historical materialism, as we shall see, but it is not identical with it. In fact, there is not even an exact name for it. Somatic (bodily) or anthropological materialism might do at a stretch, but neither term is quite satisfactory. As a way of seeing, it takes seriously what is most palpable about men and women – their animality, their practical activity and corporeal constitution. Seen from this standpoint, a good deal of philosophy looks like a suppression of the obvious. It was this that moved Friedrich Nietzsche to enquire why no philosopher had ever spoken with proper reverence of the human nose. It is to this approach that we can now turn.

CHAPTER TWO

Do Badgers Have Souls?

Ludwig Wittgenstein remarks in his *Philosophical Investigations* that if you want an image of the soul, you should take a look at the human body.[1] He means, one takes it, the body in action rather than the body as object. Practice constitutes the body rather in the sense that, for Wittgenstein, the meaning of a sign is its use. The human body is a project, a medium of signification, a point from which a world is organised. It is a mode of agency, a form of communion and interaction with others, a way of being with them rather than simply alongside them. Bodies are open-ended, unfinished, always capable of more activity than they may be manifesting right now. And all this is true of the human body as such, regardless of whether it is male or female, white or black, gay or straight, young or old. One can see, then, why this particular view of the body is not much in vogue with the fans of human difference and the apologists for the cultural constructedness of things.

Maurice Merleau-Ponty, for whom the body is our habitual way of having a world, remarks that 'having a body is, for a living creature, to be interinvolved in a definite environment, to identify oneself with certain projects and to be continually committed to them'.[2] Or, as Marx did and didn't say, the self is a relation to its surroundings (did and didn't, because he wrote this sentence in one of his works but deleted it in manuscript).[3] The body lies at the source of the various ways we are bound up with one other, which is why the word can be used to denote a collective phenomenon ('a body of ferocious Corsican pirates') as well as an individual one. It is what gives us a field of activity, a field which is in no sense external to it. In *On Certainty*, Wittgenstein professed himself puzzled by the phrase 'the external world'. 'External to what?' is perhaps what he had in mind. Certainly not to ourselves. Because we are incarnate creatures, we are as much in the world as are our sewage systems. The world is not an object set over against us, to be contemplated from some elusive location within our skulls.

Among other more glamorous things, bodies are material objects, and the ultimate objectification of the flesh is known as death. It is worth noting, however, that Thomas Aquinas, like his mentor Aristotle, refuses to use the word 'body' of a corpse. He speaks instead of the remains of a body, as we sometimes do ourselves. A dead body is only a body in a manner of speaking. As Denys Turner remarks, it is not as though 'a dead person is a person in the unfortunate condition of being dead'.[4] It is simply part of the damage inflicted by a Cartesian heritage that when we hear the phrase 'the body in the library', the last thing that springs to mind is an assiduous reader. Imagine someone ringing you up and asking, 'Is George there?' It would make sense to reply, 'Yes, but he's asleep', but it would sound odd to say, 'Yes, but he's dead'. To say that George is dead is to say that he is not there; and for Aristotle and Aquinas the reason why he is not there is because his body is not there, even if the remains of it are. A gravestone marks the spot where someone is no longer present. The material remains of George may be sprawled on the living room floor or stuffed into the sideboard, but the active, expressive, communicative, relational, self-realising body that was the earthly George is no longer around. His corpse is not a different mode of being George, but a matter of not being George at all.

You might also ring up knowing that George was alive and ask, 'Is George's body there?' This, too, would sound odd, just as it seems strange to speak of 'the body of the teapot' rather than just the teapot. It makes it sound as though there is something more to the teapot than its material constitution. Similarly, 'George's body' makes it sound as though there is something more to George than his body, which is not the case. We are only tempted to imagine so because George is a body of a certain (active, relational, communicative etc.)

kind. But all this is part of what it means to be a human body, not a set of properties superadded to it. It belongs to such bodies to surpass themselves. There is something more to a copy of *Mansfield Park* than print, but not in the sense that there is print plus something else (images, for example) on the page.

Bodies as material objects are not much in fashion in these culturalist times. Even so, it is worth recalling that whatever else human beings may be, they are lumps of matter or natural objects, and that anything more subtle or sexy they can get up to must occur within this context. Objectification is by no means always to be regretted. It happens every time we enter into a relationship with each other, or with some aspect of the world. If men and women differ from parcels of matter like gooseberries and shovels, it is not because they conceal some mysterious entity inside themselves, but because they are chunks of matter of a highly specific kind – a specificity which mind-language or soul-language seeks rather misleadingly to pin down. They are not lumps of natural stuff with some ghostly appendage attached to them, but mounds of material which are inherently active, creative, communicative, relational, self-expressive, self-realising, world-transforming and self-transcendent (which is to say, historical). All of this just *is* their soul. Soul-language is simply a way of distinguishing between bodies of this type (or of some other animal kind) and bodies such as pitchforks or bottles of brown sauce.

Like Aristotle, Aquinas and Wittgenstein regard the soul as the 'form' of the body – as its animating principle or peculiar mode of self-organisation. This is not an especially mysterious affair. It is perfectly open to view. The fury in another's face, Wittgenstein remarks, is there as clearly as in your own breast.[5] Marx speaks of the other being 'present in his sensuous immediacy' to us.[6] You can see someone's soul just as you can see their grief or rage. In fact, to see their grief or rage *is* to see their soul. 'My attitude towards him,' Wittgenstein writes, 'is an attitude towards a soul. I am not of the *opinion* that he has a soul.'[7] So much for the prejudice that consciousness is private. It is not as though I need to deliberate with myself whether he is a sentient being before deciding not to shoot him in the head. Only very clever people, as Wittgenstein might sardonically put it, check up on whether you have a soul before inviting you out to lunch. Our consciousness, to use a term of which Wittgenstein is properly sceptical, is inscribed on our bodies rather in the way that the meaning is present in a word. We are not present in our bodies in the way that a soldier squats in a tank. In this sense, the body itself is a kind of sign. As Jean-Luc Nancy remarks, it is 'a sign of itself', rather than of some reality distinct from it.[8]

It belongs to such anti-dualist thought to deny that we are always certain of our own experience but have to guess at the experience of others, or deduce what they are feeling from their behaviour. On the contrary, there are times when we can be unsure of what we ourselves are feeling (is this anxiety or irritation?) and perfectly sure of what someone else is going through. He is uttering those agonising shrieks because his right leg has just been shot off. One does not 'infer' that he is in torment from seeing him thrash helplessly around, any more than a reader familiar with the word 'microlepidoptera' 'infers' on coming across it that it means the kind of small moths which are of interest only to specialists. In most instances, we do not feel our way tentatively from the physical sign to the inner meaning. The two are given together, like body and soul. This is not to say that our behaviour is always luminously transparent, any more than the meaning of a sign is always self-evident. There may well be enigmas and equivocations, twilight cases and intractable problems of interpretation; but this is not because the meaning of what we do is private, or buried too deeply within our behaviour to be easily extracted. It is not buried within it at all.

Emotions are bound up with our needs, interests, aims, intentions and so on, all of which are in turn bound up with our participation in the public world. It is not invariably helpful to speak of such sentiments as being 'inside' us. Howling, snarling or smashing bottles of Scotch over people's heads are not internal affairs. We can, of course, hide what we are thinking or feeling, but this is a complex social practice we have to learn, rather as we have to learn to be insincere. That infants cannot conceal the fact that they are wet or hungry is one of Nature's less agreeable inventions. Chimpanzees can lie, in the sense of signalling information they know to be false; but unlike Hollywood celebrities or spokespersons for the CIA they cannot be insincere, since insincerity involves maintaining a façade at odds with one's actual feelings, and to pull off such an intricate operation requires the resources of language. That they cannot engage in outrageously hypocritical behaviour, however, is no unqualified compliment to chimpanzees, since a creature who cannot be insincere cannot be sincere either. Meaning what you say is only possible if you are capable of not meaning it.

In Wittgenstein's view, we would not be able to learn the names for emotions and sensations if everyone concealed them all the time. (There are those who regard the English as an exception to this truth.) If nobody ever acted out their emotions – if there was only grief, but not grief behaviour – the discourse of human emotion would never get off the ground. There is a necessary relation between what we feel and our physical manifestations of it. Grief behaviour is a criterion for the proper application of the word 'grief', part of how we grasp the meaning of the word; and it is by picking up the public use of the word that I can identify a feeling of my own as falling into this category of sentiments. If the relation between feeling grief and grief behaviour were purely contingent, everyone could be undergoing an utterly unique experience when they collapse howling to the carpet, and we would have no language of psychology in common. In this sense, it is the body that helps to save us from the false gods of private meaning and the solitary ego.

We can see that tractors and hairdryers do not have souls simply by looking at what they do, or rather at what they don't do. We do not need to peer into their innards to establish the fact. Indeed, to claim that they do not have souls is to claim that they do not have such innards – that they lack the complex depths manifest in the behaviour of, say, Judi Dench, though less evidently so in the case of Lindsay Lohan. It is important to recognise, however, that if Judi Dench has complex depths, it is not because she was born with them, as one might be born with a missing finger or a mole on one's shoulder, but by virtue of her participation in a practical form of life. 'Consciousness' just *is* such a participation.

If the soul or self is distinct from the body, it can always be misperceived as the sovereign lord of it. To view it as the form of the body, however, suggests that we cannot speak of our relation to our bodies as one of proprietorship. Who, for one thing, would be doing the owning? There may be some good arguments for abortion, but the belief that one's body is one's private property, to be disposed of as one wishes, is not one of them. I did not manufacture my own body, but derive my flesh from others. 'It is clear,' Marx comments, '. . . that individuals certainly make one another, physically and mentally, but do not make themselves.'[9] It is true that one can speak of using one's body. 'If I had the use of my body I would throw it out of the window', Samuel Beckett's Malone reflects glumly. I might stretch my limbs selflessly across a stream so that you can scramble across my spine without getting your Victoria Beckham skirt wet; but one does not deploy one's body as an instrument from some point of mastery or possession outside it. Jean-Jacques Rousseau argues somewhat paradoxically that it is the fact that we are not masters of ourselves which allows us to be autonomous. If the self is not ours to own, we cannot yield it up to another. Besides, if we are masters of ourselves, then it follows that we are also our own slaves.

To communicate with you by phone or email is to be bodily present to you, though not physically so. Physical presence would involve sharing the same material space. If an activity does not involve my body, it does not involve me. Thinking is as much a corporeal affair as drinking. Thomas Aquinas rejects the Platonic prejudice that the less our actions involve the body, the more admirable they are.[10] In his view, our bodies are constitutive of all our activities, however 'spiritual' or high-minded they may be. For Aquinas, we are animals all the way through, not just from the neck down. We are, to be sure, social, rational and historical beings as well, but the materialist point is that we are these things in a peculiarly animal way. They are not alternatives to our animality, or accessories to it. History, culture and society are specific modes of creatureliness, not ways of transcending it. Animal bodies are inherently self-transcendent.

'Mind' or 'soul', then, is a way of describing how a certain species of animality is constituted, its distinctive way of being alive. In this sense, there is no problem in shifting from the body to the soul, since to say 'body' in the sense of animal is already to say 'soul'. As Alasdair MacIntyre comments, 'our whole initial bodily comportment to the world is originally an animal comportment',[11] a state of affairs that our later accession to language does nothing to liquidate. Aquinas teaches that human rationality is animal rationality. We need to be able to reason in order to survive and flourish as material creatures. We are cognitive beings because we are carnal ones. Nietzsche thought this to be so, while Marx speaks of our 'sensuous consciousness'.[12] If our thought is discursive, in the sense of unfolding in time, it is because our sensory life is discursive as well. Angels, being bodiless, are a different proposition. In fact, Aquinas does not regard angels as rational beings at all. This is not to suggest that the Archangel Gabriel is off his head, simply that the language game of rationality does not apply to him any more than it does to a jar of pickles. John Milton, for whom angels are incarnate beings who merge their bodies completely together in the act of sex, takes a different view.

Human identity is a corporeal affair. Aquinas would have believed in the existence of the disembodied soul of Michael

Jackson, but he would not have considered it to be Michael Jackson. It is, so to speak, Michael Jackson standing by to become himself again by being bodily transformed at the general resurrection, rather more dramatically than in his numerous corporeal reincarnations when alive. (Wittgenstein, incidentally, is wryly amused by the idea of the soul 'leaving' the body at death. How can something immaterial leave something material? He also notes the absurdity of supposing that eternity will begin when I die. How can eternity begin?) One of the dangers of viewing the self as a disembodied soul is that you may then feel free to treat other people as soulless bodies. If the body is just a spiritless chunk of stuff, there is nothing especially amiss with frequenting brothels or exploiting slave labour. You are not damaging anyone's soul in doing so – assuming that slaves have a soul in the first place, which many a slave-owner has taken leave to doubt. Thomas Hardy's Tess Durbeyfield, a woman whose body is plundered by others for both sexual and economic profit, finally resorts to the desperate tactic of dissociating herself from it altogether, severing it from what Hardy calls her living will. Schizophrenia, a condition in which one may feel one's body as an alien appendage, can be a last-ditch survival strategy in a predatory world.

The soul for Aquinas is simply the specific way in which a creature is organised, how its form of life differs from that of other organisms. Marx will later find himself in agreement. In this sense, it is ironic that most of those who commend difference and specificity are uninterested in the idea. 'The whole character of a species,' Marx declares, '. . . resides in the nature of its life activity, and free conscious activity constitutes the species-character of man.'[13] The more tender-hearted readers of this book will thus be delighted to learn that badgers do indeed have souls, since they enjoy a peculiar form of material existence, though their soul differs from that of a slug or a member of the Republican Party. What would cause Aquinas some disquiet, however, is the idea that badgers or human beings 'have' souls, which are 'united' to their bodies. It was this species of Platonism that he disputed, and he got into hot water with the ecclesiastical authorities for doing so. As Maurice Merleau-Ponty writes, 'the union of body and soul is not an amalgamation between two mutually external terms, subject and object, brought about by arbitrary decree. It is enacted at every instant in the movement of existence.'[14] It is our life that deconstructs the difference between the two, which is not necessarily to claim that they melt into harmony with one another. We have seen already that it belongs to the expressive body to be capable of objectifying itself, conscious of its flesh as to some extent unmasterable and opaque. It is just that we do not feel the body's resistance to spirit from some disembodied point within it.

* * *

One of the greatest of all Christian theologians, then, turns out to be in some respects a full-blooded materialist. This is not entirely surprising, since Christianity itself is in some sense a materialist creed. The doctrine of the Incarnation means that God is an animal. He is present in the Eucharist in the everyday stuff of bread and wine, in the mundane business of chewing and digesting. Salvation is not primarily a matter of cult and ritual but of feeding the hungry and tending the sick. Jesus spends much of his time restoring damaged human bodies to health, along with a number of deranged minds. Love is a material practice, not a spiritual sentiment. Its paradigm is the love of strangers and enemies, which is unlikely to generate much of a warm glow. Wittgenstein remarks provocatively that 'love is not a feeling', though, as it happens, it is not the proper anonymity of charity that he has in mind.[15] He means that love is not something you might feel for only eight seconds, as you might feel pain. It would not make sense to say, 'That couldn't have been pain, or it wouldn't have passed off so quickly', but it would make sense to say it of love. You cannot be violently in love with someone only for the length of time it takes to put the cat out. Love is dispositional, situational, embedded in a context and narrative. Even so, though Wittgenstein is not thinking of the Christian gospel here, 'love is not a feeling' is a proposition it would most certainly endorse.

Materiality is blessed for Christianity because it is God's creation. James Joyce was a devotee of Aquinas, and *Ulysses*, a novel to which nothing corporeal is alien, is in some sense a Thomist text. The Christian belief is in the resurrection of the body, not the immortality of the soul. The sexual coupling of bodies is in St Paul's view a foretaste of the kingdom of God. The Holy Spirit is not some sacred spook but a dynamic force that shatters and transforms the face of the earth. Faith is not a solitary mental state but a conviction which springs from sharing in the practical, communal life-form known as the Church. It is folly to high-minded Greeks, a carnivalesque affair which pits the common life against hermetic ideas, exalting the lowly and toppling the mighty from their thrones. It consists primarily in a commitment to the death, not in a set of theoretical propositions. Even Friedrich Nietzsche, who considered Christianity to be the greatest catastrophe ever to befall humanity, thought that to reduce it 'to a holding something to be true, to a mere phenomenality of consciousness', was to travesty it.[16] At its centre is a lowly itinerant who excoriates the rich and powerful and consorts with crooks and whores. Since his solidarity with the poor constitutes a thorn in the flesh of the priestly and political elite, he ends up suffering the kind of grisly death reserved by the Roman imperial power for political rebels.

Aquinas has a somewhat more subtle conception of matter than the mechanical materialists. As Denys Turner puts it, his objection to such materialists 'was that they were simply not very good on the subject of matter'.[17] There is, Turner remarks, 'a lot more to matter itself than meets the eye of today's average materialist'.[18] Human beings, he writes, are in Aquinas's view 'matter articulate, stuff that speaks'.[19] 'Today's materialists,' he complains, 'believe that matter is all there is, and that matter is meaninglessly dumb, for all meaning is talk *about* matter, none of it matter talking.'[20]

The body, then, is meaningful matter, a point which applies to dingoes as much as to humans. Practical intelligence is for the most part bodily intelligence. A small child who has yet to acquire speech reaches out to grab a toy, and the gesture is inherently meaningful. It belongs, one might claim, to a layer of somatic, pre-verbal signification inscribed in our very flesh. The meaning clings to the action like a lining to a sleeve. It is built into the material gesture. It is not just a question of an observer's interpretation of the act. Neither is it a matter of the child's own conception, since he or she lacks as yet the means to formulate one. Yet, if the body is articulate matter, isn't this also true of a hosepipe or a garden gnome? Hosepipes are not of course capable of speech, but they are bits of articulate matter in the sense of being significantly structured. However, it is human beings who design them, imprinting the dumb stuff of rubber and metal with intentionality, shaping them to perform a function. In any case, the human body is not just inscribed with meaning; unlike garden gnomes, it is also the source of it.

In Aquinas's view, matter is the principle of individuation. What makes you yourself rather than someone else is the particular hunk of material you happen to be. Indeed, 'body' can be an archaic term for 'person', as in 'the housekeeper was a neat, bright-eyed little body'. In such quaint usages, a non-Cartesian conception of the human person lingers on. The usage, however, can also be mildly misleading, since to have a human body is a condition of being a person, not synonymous with it. The body is given, whereas becoming a person is an arduous historical project, to be superbly, atrociously or indifferently executed. The fact remains, however, that for Aquinas I am not myself because I have a certain generic type of body or soul, but because of the particular parcel of flesh I am made up of. It is this that marks off one member of a species from another. If human souls differ from each other, it is because they animate different bodies. What individuates us, however, also gathers us into one. To have a human body is to enjoy a form of solidarity with other creatures of one's kind.

Aquinas is an epistemological materialist as well as a somatic one. In his view, the whole of our knowledge springs from our engagement with material reality. Talk of God, for example, is derived analogically from what we know of the world around us. If metaphor, as he maintains, is the mode of discourse most appropriate to human beings, it is because it casts meaning into sensory mode, which is where we fleshly types feel most at home. For all his insistence on the senses, however, Aquinas does not hold with the empiricists that the mind is simply a passive receptacle of so-called sense data. On the contrary, he teaches that the intellect actively makes sense of reality, and is thus a form of practice in itself.

There is a parallel here between the epistemologies of Aquinas and Marx. Aquinas sees any particular 'sense datum' as an abstraction from the complex concreteness of our experience as a whole. As Denys Turner puts it, 'the intellect draws together in acts of understanding the "abstract" experience of each of the senses, thereby grasping the concrete and dense realities wherein is found their meaning'.[21] Marx writes in similar vein in the *Grundrisse* of the human understanding as 'rising' from the abstract to the concrete. We generally think of the abstract as lofty and abstruse and the concrete as simple and commonplace, but both thinkers stand this antithesis on its head. Thought for Marx begins with abstract categories such as money, which to his mind are simple notions, and then proceeds to synthesise them into such complex realities as a historical mode of production. It is these phenomena that are truly concrete, a word which literally means the convergence of different features.

Alligators, too, are meaningful bits of matter, and reason is not confined to humanity. Other animals are capable of it as well, as Aquinas readily allows. Indeed, in his view, to be animal is to be rational. Reason is just the kind of faculty appropriate to such organic forms of life, in contrast to, say, the intellect of an angel. A wolfhound can be guided by beliefs and reasons. It may not be able to open a savings account or join the Girl Guides, but it can certainly conclude that since a walk is off the agenda it might as well save its breath and stop barking. Its capacity to reason, however, is largely confined to its immediate surroundings, which is also true of toddlers. Toddlers can reason, but they cannot come up with propositions of Einsteinian splendour. Nor can a dog critically evaluate its own behaviour, a self-monitoring which requires the sort of self-reflexivity only language can provide. It cannot, in a word, be a moral animal, any more than an infant can be. (Or God, for that matter, whom no reputable theologian would regard as a moral being.) Babies cannot ask themselves whether they might have been better off not being born, though their elder siblings may well have an opinion on the question. A mother bird cannot argue herself out of the instinct that impels her to feed her fledglings. She cannot be struck by the existential futility of the whole project and fly off to the Bahamas instead.

What makes the difference for Aquinas is that human beings are linguistic as well as sensory animals. It is this which is the primary mark of our rationality. Our sensations are mediated by language, as a snail's are not; and it is this above all that allows us a degree of self-distance, and thus of critical self-reflection. The sign-systems of dolphins are impressively intricate, but it is hard not to feel that they are overshadowed by the works of Proust. Language allows us to be more intimate with each other than mere physical contiguity.

Lovers who chat long into the night are closer than those who simply have sex. By the same token, however, linguistic animals can wreak far more havoc than non-linguistic ones. Squirrels cannot commit genocide, unless they are being remarkably furtive about it. Their thinking is too close to the bone for that. But they cannot come up with *Don Giovanni* either, and for much the same reasons. Giorgio Agamben argues in *The Open* that humanity is constituted by distancing, mastering and destroying its own animality, but he fails to say enough about how this self-objectifying can be a source of value as well as a cause of calamity.[22]

In the *Philosophical Investigations*, Wittgenstein famously declares that if a lion could speak, we would not be able to understand what it said.[23] Could we not find a translator fluent in Lionese and don a pair of headphones? Not in Wittgenstein's view. For him, a lion's material form of life is simply too remote from ours for dialogue to be possible. Because of its physiology, a lion does not organise the world in the way we do. In *The Will to Power*, Friedrich Nietzsche similarly assumes that the other animals inhabit spheres alien to our own, and consequently shows no interest in chatting up penguins. Like Aquinas, he believes that we think as we do because of the kind of bodies we have. A different kind of body would yield us a different kind of world. Wittgenstein, however, may be wrong in assuming that such realms are mutually incommensurate. Alasdair MacIntyre, for example, claims that if dolphins could speak, those who are expert in their ways might well be able to understand them.[24] For Martin Heidegger, too, there is some overlap between our own world and that of non-linguistic creatures – a case encapsulated in his portentous declaration that 'the dog ... does go up the stairs with us'.[25] (There is something irresistibly amusing about Heidegger, with his oracular tone and mouth-filling philosophical style, speaking of going upstairs with a dog.)

Whatever our differences from the beasts, our own forms of reasoning are in Aquinas's view deeply embedded in our animal nature, which is one reason why he is by no means the arid rationalist that some have taken him to be. Because our thought is enmeshed with our sensory and emotional exist- ence, it is bound to differ from the 'thought' of a brainy computer, which has no sensory or emotional life for its 'mind' to be enmeshed with. The earliest goods of human beings, by contrast, are material and emotional ones: warmth, sleep, dryness, breast milk, human contact, freedom from discom- fort and so on. From this humble root grows the infant's speechless gratitude to its carers, which in turn lays the seedbed of what we know as morality. It is on this flesh-and-blood foundation that we eventually come to think, and our thought will continue to be underpinned by it. It is true, however, that if we think elaborately enough we can come to overlook this material and emotional infrastructure, a condition commonly known as philosophy.

Reasoning is interwoven with our practical projects, but those projects are not themselves purely rational affairs. The final goal of all human activity is happiness or well-being; but although the fatiguing business of learning how to be fulfilled involves reason, it is not reducible to it. This is not because rationality is a clinical, dispassionate matter. To be reasonable is to strive to view a situation as it really is, a strenuous enterprise which involves lifting our gaze above our endemic narcissism and self-interest.[26] It also requires patience, persistence, resourcefulness, honesty, humility, the courage to confess that one is mistaken, a readiness to trust others, a refusal of anodyne fantasies and self-serving illusions, an acceptance of what may run counter to our own interests and so on. In this sense, objectivity is a moral affair. It has nothing to do with some bloodless disinterestedness. On the contrary, it is in our interests to be rational. It may even be a question of our survival. To be open to the reality of a situation is to manifest a selfless concern for it, and a selfless concern for what lies beyond the boisterous ego is traditionally known as love. Love and knowledge are in this sense allied, an affinity most obvious when it comes to knowledge of other persons. We can know others only through their voluntary self-disclosure, which in turn involves trust, which is itself a species of love.

Like thoughts, feelings can be either rational or irrational. They can be appropriate to the nature of their object, or they can be disproportionate to it, as with sentimentalism. It is rational to mourn the death of a loved one, but irrational to leap off a cliff when your pet hamster finally breathes its last. Even so, reason does not go all the way down. It is true that unless you can offer reasons why you love someone, it is hard to see how you yourself can know that you do. One must be able to come up with grounds for one's affection for another person: that she has an enormous amount of money, that she makes Kate Winslet look like King Kong, that she is remarkably tolerant of shiftless, narcissistic men, and so on. All the same, the collusion between love and reason is not complete. A third party, after all, could acknowledge the force of your reasoning without being in love with her himself. Love and well-being finally transcend reason, but they founder if they throw it to the winds. The same is true of the relations between reason and faith.

A rationality ungrounded in practical, sensory existence is not simply defective: it is not truly rational at all. Reason unhinged from the senses is a form of madness, as King Lear discovers. One name for what we might call sensuous reasoning is the aesthetic, which first sees the light of day not as talk about art but as a discourse of the body.[27] It represents an attempt on the part of a rather bloodless form of Enlightenment reason to incorporate what one might call the logic of the senses. Modern aesthetics begins life as an attempt to smuggle the body back into a form of rationality that is in danger of expelling it as so much excess baggage. It is in the work of art above all that the rational and the sensory work conspire fruitfully together. Yet the aesthetic is not simply a supplement to reason, as the Enlightenment tended to believe. Without acknowledging its source in sensory life, reason cannot be properly rational in the first place. A distinctively human rationality is one responsive to the needs and confines of the flesh.

There is more to the relation between reason and aesthetics than this. The work of art is also a model of what Aristotle terms praxis, meaning the kind of activities whose goods are internal to them.[28] Unless you are as talented as Joshua Bell, there is no point to playing the violin beyond the type of fulfilment peculiar to the activity itself. It is a self-grounding, self-constituting, self-validating form of practice. Laughing, joking, dancing, making love, playing the tin whistle, collecting insanely expensive porcelain soap dishes and drinking yourself under the table do not get you anywhere. The rationality that governs them is not an instrumental one. One does not treat such activities simply as a means to an end distinct from them, like smashing a car windscreen in order to remove a Louis Vuitton handbag from the passenger seat. It is true that art may be instrumental in the sense of enriching one's sense of human existence, but it can do so successfully only if one's attention is unwaveringly focused on the artwork itself – on what Marx would call its use-value, as opposed to its exchange-value. Its meaning and value are inseparable from its actual performance, which in Aristotle's eyes is also true of the practice of virtue.

Generally speaking, these kinds of activity are the most precious ones. It is true that some instrumental actions are just as estimable (feeding the hungry, for example), and without instrumental rationality of some kind we would never be able to rid the world of chemical weapons. Nor would most of us be able to get out of bed, an indispensable condition for ridding the world of chemical weapons. Even so, most of our finest accomplishments carry their ends within themselves. To use a theological idiom again, they exist simply for the hell of it. When we engage in such ventures, we are at our most reasonable. Reason ceases to be a mere tool or calculative device and becomes a form of self-realisation to be valued for its own sake.

To act instrumentally, by contrast, risks skimming over the sensuous, affective qualities of things in the name of attaining some goal. We do not linger lovingly over the shape and texture of our railway ticket before reluctantly yielding it up to the inspector. For Marxism, capitalism involves a consumerist orgy of the senses; yet it is also, paradoxically, a fleshless, ascetic style of existence, as material objects are stripped of their bulk and reduced to the abstract status of commodities. A similar abstraction befalls the human body, as we shall see in a moment. Bertolt Brecht dreamed of a future in which thought might become a real sensuous pleasure; and socialists in general anticipate a time when instrumental reason, while still wholly indispensable to human affairs, will exert less of a despotic sway over our lives. Radical political thought is indeed in the service of political practice; but that practice aims for a condition in which we might be freer to enjoy reasoning for its own sake. Those socialists who tout a brand of left-utilitarianism (theory can be justified only if it issues in practical change, preferably within the next few hours) fail to see that we would be truly emancipated only when we no longer felt the need to apologise for the exercise of reason before some grim-faced tribunal of historical utility.

CHAPTER THREE

Emancipating the Senses

THERE IS NO evidence that Karl Marx was indebted to Thomas Aquinas, though Friedrich Nietzsche quotes the saintly theologian at length in *On the Genealogy of Morals*. Marx was not the most ardent fan of medieval theology. Even so, we have seen already that there are some intriguing parallels between the two thinkers, which can probably be ascribed to the fact that they both came under the influence of Aristotle. Marx, too, is a somatic materialist whose starting point is active, sensuous, practical human life. He is not concerned with ontological materialism, in the sense of asking what the world is made of, and would doubtless have dismissed the issue as idly metaphysical. He had a brisk way with what he saw as fancy ideas. Like Nietzsche and Wittgenstein, Marx was a philosopher with a deep-seated scorn for philosophising. His colleague Friedrich Engels was a materialist in a standard philosophical sense of the term, but Marx himself was not. For him, the field of materialist enquiry was history and society.

In taking the approach he did, Marx saw himself as inaugurating a new style of materialism. All previous materialism, he claims in the first of his theses on Feuerbach, has made the mistake of conceiving of 'the thing, reality, sensuousness . . . only in the form of the object or of contemplation, but not as sensuous human activity, not subjectively'.[1] His compatriot Ludwig Feuerbach was right, he maintains, to start from the corporeal nature of humanity. The problem was that he did not grasp this nature as active. For him, as for the empiricists, the senses remain essentially passive organs, whereas for Marx they are constitutive features of human practice, modes of engagement with the world. It is true that the empiricists base knowledge and activity on the body, as Marx does himself; the problem in his view is simply that they have a false conception of the body. Terms like 'sense data' and 'sense impressions', not to speak of the quaint notion of concepts as images in one's head, betray a reified view of what it is to be flesh and blood. Wittgenstein will later query the idea that our senses somehow 'inform' us or yield us 'evidence' of our surroundings. Besides, in its stubborn loyalty to the senses, empiricist thought finds it hard to explain how one steps from there to ideas. If there is too little of the body in rationalism, there is too much of it in empiricism.

Marx even speaks of the senses as being 'theoreticians in their immediate praxis',[2] meaning that, like theoretical reflection, they are able to relate to objects for their own sake, rather than for some functional end. The model for this is the aesthetic. To see something aesthetically is generally assumed to mean seeing it contemplatively; but for Marx the true opposition is not between the practical and the aesthetic, but between both of them on the one hand and the instrumental or utilitarian on the other. We respect the specific qualities of things, which is the province of the aesthetic, when we employ those things for the practical ends for which they were fashioned. It is this that Marx means by use-value. So the practical and the aesthetic are closely allied, which is not how we usually think of the matter. Exchange-value and instrumental reason, by contrast, use objects simply as means to an end, with scant regard for their sensuous specificity.[3] In this sense, for all their practical orientation, they are de-materialising forces.

Our sensory capacities, Marx argues, are not fixed and given, but have a complex history of their own. They evolve as humanity sets to work on the material world, transforming its own sensory constitution in the process. The body, a natural phenomenon, is thus also a social product, as are most of the things we see, touch and taste. 'Even the objects of the simplest "sensuous certainty",' Marx writes in *The German Ideology*, 'are only given [to humanity] through social development, industry and commercial intercourse.'[4] He seems momentarily to have forgotten that stars, waterfalls, mountain goats and the like are objects of sensuous certainty but not social products. The history of industry, in the broadest sense of that term, is 'the open book of the essential powers of humanity, human psychology present in tangible form'.[5] It is as though the history of human self-production, in a sense of the term that includes smelling a rose and eating a peach, is the material body in which the human spirit is incarnate. What from one viewpoint is an accumulation of productive forces is also, viewed from another angle, the story of the human sensorium. Sensory capabilities and social institutions are sides of the same coin.

The relationship between them, however, has been a troubled one. A number of key Marxist concepts – fetishism, reification, alienation, commodification – mark a problem in this area. In a curious disturbance in the relations between matter and spirit, fetishism, phantasm and abstraction are in Marx's view built into the structure of social reality, and can come to exert an uncanny power over it. We are dealing here with efficacious illusions, not idle fancies. There are few activities more palpable than labour; yet even this, so Marx claims, becomes abstract under capitalist conditions, as one works less to produce specific objects than to generate a profit. Commodities, too, are abstract phenomena, pure media of exchange; yet in a market society their interactions really do determine the destiny of flesh-and-blood individuals. A fluctuation on the stock exchange can throw thousands out of work. Ideology may trade in wraiths and phantoms, yet if it thereby distracts us from the need for political change, it is real enough.

Even the most basic of sensory activities presuppose a good deal of material stage-setting. Behind our touching and tasting lies a whole chronicle of human commerce with the world. Feuerbach, by contrast, fails to see the material reality around him as sensuously *produced*, and thus as social and historical. If such production were suspended for only a year, Marx comments sardonically, Feuerbach would soon find that the whole human world had lapsed from existence, along with himself. His own starting point, by contrast, is not simply the material nature of humanity, but men and women as material *agents*. Deploying a surfeit of adjectives, he speaks of human individuals as 'corporeal, living, real, sensuous, objective' beings.[6] They are active bodies rather than thinking things, creatures who know the world only as it manifests itself within the context of their practical activities. As Jürgen Habermas writes, 'the objectivity of the possible objects of experience is [for Marx] grounded in the identity of a natural substratum, namely that of the bodily organisation of man, which is oriented towards action'.[7]

Labour for Marx, or production more generally, is thus an epistemological category as well as a social and economic one. What for the philosopher are possible objects of experience are for the materialist the fruits of productive activity, and it is this that guarantees their objectivity. We know things through the process of fashioning them. So it is that Marx develops what Habermas calls 'an anthropological theory of cognition'.[8] It is not in the first place thought or language which gives us a world, but the world-constitutive powers of production, in a rich, capacious sense of that term, with which thought and language are bound up.

To begin from human agency is to dismantle the distinction between subjects and objects, since practice is a material, objective affair, yet one inscribed with spirit (motives, values, purposes, interpretations and so on). It is also to relax the tension between Nature and history, given that the body belongs to both spheres simultaneously. Marx points up its ambivalent status when he writes of both material and sexual production as being doubled in this respect.[9] 'The production of life,' he writes, 'both of one's own in labour and of fresh life in procreation . . . appears as a double relationship: on the one hand as a natural, on the other as a social relationship.'[10] Humanity, he observes, has 'an historical nature and a natural history'.[11] If he refuses to collapse culture into Nature, he is aware that to collapse Nature into culture is quite as reductionist a move.

Marx may begin from human beings as material agents, but it is not exactly where he ends up. The later author of *Capital* continues to believe that political emancipation concerns such flesh-and-blood creatures, but it does not follow from this that one's analysis should begin from them. In fact, *Capital* is not concerned with individuals at all. It treats them for its diagnostic purposes purely as the 'bearers' of certain social and economic structures. In the light of this, it might be argued that the early Marx does not start far back enough. Simply for us to be social agents, an enormous amount of material infrastructure must already be in place. Indeed, Marx himself complains that idealist thought fails to start far back enough. One can begin with ideas, but then where do ideas come from? What must already have happened for men and women to be capable of reflection? What forces put human subjects in place? These, by and large, are not legitimate questions for those for whom consciousness constitutes an absolute origin or ground. One could try to dig beneath this ground, they might maintain, but to do so would itself involve consciousness. So one would be guilty of what is technically known as a *petitio principii*, presupposing what one was seeking to explain.

Not all of his acolytes endorse Marx's case about agency. In *On Materialism*, Sebastiano Timpanaro thinks that the *maître* is mistaken to claim that we relate to Nature only through our historical activity. There is a passive dimension to the relationship as well. As we have seen already, our bodily nature is the source of our agency, but also of our susceptibility to harm. To say that we are mortal is to say that our bodies bear within them the seeds of their ultimate undoing. To see men and women as active, world-producing animals is to restore to them the dignity which mechanical materialism denies them, while to be aware of their vulnerability prevents that vision from becoming overweening. Timpanaro recalls us to such features of the human condition as 'the brevity and frailty of human existence, the contrast between the smallness and weakness of man and the infinity of the cosmos . . . the debility produced by age . . . the fear of one's own death and sorrow at the death of others'.[12] He also rejects as 'idealist sophistry' the view that since biology is always socially mediated, the biological is nothing and the social is everything. To 'idealist sophistry' one might add 'culturalist cant'. The fact that bleeding to death may be differently construed by different cultures does not mean that one is not bleeding to death. No doubt it is gratifying to the apostles of cultural relativism that we die in such a fascinating variety of ways, but it would be even more gratifying if we did not die at all.

Marx is aware of the body as mortal, suffering and conditioned by factors beyond its control. He speaks in an early work of death as the way the species bears in upon the individual. Even so, agency is fundamental to his conception of humanity. As the Scottish philosopher John Macmurray comments, 'Our knowledge of the world is primarily an aspect of our action in the world.'[13] For Marx, the primary form this action takes is labour. Men and women can survive only by working upon their environment, and it is the peculiar constitution of their bodies that allows them to do so. The fact that they are linguistic animals, for example, means that they can launch the kind of collaborative projects they need in order to reproduce their material life. What is central for Marx, then, is what he calls 'the physical organisation [of human beings] . . . and their consequent relation to the rest of Nature', a Nature which he describes at one point as 'man's inorganic body'.[14] The writing of history, he insists, 'must always set out from these natural bases and their modification in the course of history through the action of men'.[15] It is the body that lies at the root of human history. Human beings manifest a material nature (or 'species being', as Marx calls it) which includes the capacity to realise and reproduce themselves, and in doing so to transform their conditions of existence. It is this that is meant by having a history.

The paradox, then, is that it is because of their given anthropological features that humans are historical creatures. To claim that they have a distinctive nature is not to suggest that they are non-historical. On the contrary, it is to insist that they could not stop having a history if they tried – that they are historical beings invariably and without exception. Being historical is not itself historically relative. There are those who fear that this is to turn Marx into that grossly unfashionable figure, an essentialist. Yet if what is meant by this is that transformation is of our essence, not simply a contingent feature of our condition, then there is no reason why one should refuse the label. In any case, a good many anti-essentialists have also been anti-leftists. Anti-essentialism is by no means always on the side of the political angels.

The belief that certain aspects of humanity remain more or less constant is not among the most widely advertised features of Marx's thought. Instead, he is usually seen (not least by his disciples) as a full-blooded historicist – as one for whom all phenomena are historical all the way down, and thus both changing and changeable. This, gratifyingly, is not the case. It would be a pity if some momentous historical upheaval were to result in the human appetite for justice disappearing altogether. Mutability is by no means a good in itself. It is fortunate that tyrants pass away, but not that freedom fighters do as well. Not many fans of flux and process celebrate losing one's memory. Marx is indeed a historicist, but not a full-blooded one. In any case, by no means all historicism is politically radical. It has been at least as much a doctrine of the right as of the left. Placing a phenomenon in its historical context is not yet to have made a political move. Marx certainly believes in immutable realities, one of which is the need to labour. He speaks of it in *Capital* as an 'everlasting' fact of human existence. Angels and aristocrats do not need to work, and neither do peacocks, but humanity in general would perish without it. Socialism involves shortening the working day and dispensing with degrading toil, but it could not abolish the necessity to labour.

There are many features of humanity – language, death, sickness, fear, production, laughter, sexuality, grief at the loss of loved ones, the enjoyment of each other's company and so on – which are natural to the species.[16] Since they involve the kind of material beings we are, it is perverse of self-styled materialists to deny the fact. One name for the priority of Nature over culture is death. Some socialists are nervous of such claims because they might suggest that nothing in the human condition can be altered. And such 'naturalising' of the historical is a familiar device of ruling ideologies. But it does not follow from the fact that death is natural that sending one's son to Eton is as well. Kate Soper warns that to speak of, say, illness as part of the human condition is to risk reducing history to Nature, viewing the breakdown of the body as purely fated.[17] As such, it gives comfort to one's political opponents. This is rather like claiming that radicals should not speak of the Chartists or Suffragettes, since any positive talk of tradition might be mistaken for an affection for the Changing of the Guard. In any case, by no means all ideology is naturalising, and by no means all Nature is impervious to change.

It is true, all the same, that Marx's conception of the body has its limits. As Raymond Williams observes:

it is a fact about classical Marxism that it neglected, to its great cost, not only the basic human physical conditions . . .

but also the emotional conditions and situations which make up so large a part of all direct human relationship and practice. Problems of sexuality, including problematic sexuality, are among the most prominent omissions.[18]

There is some truth in this criticism, despite the fact that there are Marxist thinkers (William Morris, Reich, Fromm, Adorno, Marcuse and others, not to speak of a whole galaxy of Marxist feminists) who have written illuminatingly on these matters. It is also worth pointing out that since Williams wrote these words, the sexual body has come almost to eclipse the labouring one. Behind that shift lies a political history of both loss and gain, advance and retreat.

In Marx's eyes, then, Nature is more fundamental than history, since in the shape of our species-being it is what allows us to have history in the first place. Indeed, it is what determines that we *must* have a history. It is also more fundamental in the sense that the narratives we can construct are constrained by the kind of animals we are. By means of both labour and language, two activities that are closely interwoven, the human creature is able to extend its body across the planet by the prostheses we know as institutions. Among them is the amplifying of our bodily powers known as technology. In a pleasant conceit, Marx speaks in the *Grundrisse* of agriculture as the conversion of the soil into an extension of the body. Yet we can extend our bodies in this way only within the limits of their physical constitution. They can stretch as far as the moon, but probably not to distant stars. Even in a so-called post-human future, one in which technology has been thoroughly incorporated into the human body, it is still *this* body, with all its material constraints, that is in question; and if the process of incorporation evolves far enough, we may no longer be able to speak of a distinctively human body at all.

Nature is always mediated by culture (it turns up on menus, for example), but the materialist belief is that it is both prior to and independent of human affairs. It is not on our account that there are lizards and magnetic fields. We may depend on Nature, but Nature does not depend on us. To live in society is not to cease to live in Nature but to 'live' Nature in a specific way – by labour, for example, which invests it with human meaning. It is this relation via history to the material world, Marx maintains, that idealist philosophy banishes from its reflections. For some idealist thinkers, though by no means for all, philosophy deals in history and culture, while the natural sciences deal in Nature. Historical materialism, by contrast, seeks to think both dimensions simultaneously, without conflating the two. The relations between them are not symmetrical. Though natural needs are socially mediated, for example, not all social needs are naturally based. There is no natural foundation to one's desire to address the United Nations General Assembly dressed in a

Winnie the Pooh outfit, however much it may feel that way. There are no false natural needs, but there are plenty of false social ones – the demand for lap dancers, for example, as opposed perhaps to laptops.

In meeting our needs through material production, we generate further needs that must be satisfied in turn, and it is thus that human history unfolds. Men and women embark in this process on the most precious form of manufacture, which for Marx is not that of coalmines or cotton mills, but individuals' own self-production – one name for which is culture. The kind of animal body that is incapable of complex labour, desire (in the psychoanalytic sense) and extensive communication tends to repeat itself, constrained as it is by its biological cycle; whereas human beings can establish some distance between themselves and their biological determinants.

In doing so, they can launch themselves out on a narrative rather more adventurous than the career of the caterpillar, which viewed from a purely human standpoint appears a trifle tedious. In fact, one of Marx's complaints against class-society is that it prevents individuals from fully embarking on this fraught, perilous, exhilarating enterprise. Caught up in one form of exploitation after another, human beings have so far languished in what he calls 'pre-history', subject to social constraints that seem to confront them with all the recalcitrance of Nature itself. It is history as repetition rather than innovation. The only truly historic act, then, would be to break with these animal-like cycles and begin to construct a more open-ended narrative for ourselves. It is because such a saga would not be predictable, unlike the behaviour of a caterpillar, that Marx has strikingly little to say about the future.

To claim that Nature finally has the edge over culture is not of course to deny that the two are intertwined in practice. Labour for Marx is the key point at which they converge, as is the body itself. Sexuality, too, lies on the cusp between Nature and culture. 'Human beings,' Marx writes, 'who daily remake their own life, begin to make other human beings to propagate their kind.'[19] The inequality of gender roles, he argues, is the earliest form of the division of labour. Yet the truth is that the two domains, of Nature and culture, refuse to slot smoothly together. Labour would not be so laborious if they did. Nature is what hurts, resisting our efforts to mould it into manageable shape. And culture is always at risk of disavowing its roots in such humble stuff, like an Oedipal child who dreams of some posher provenance than its actual, embarrassingly unglamorous parents.

Yet though Marx (leaving aside a few early utopian gestures) insists on the non-identity of the two realms, few thinkers have matched his efforts to grasp them in a single thought. Nature and history have traditionally been rival objects of attention; but Marx is that rare kind of materialist who assigns a key role to human consciousness at the same time as he investigates its workaday material basis. If his concern is with politics, he does not neglect physiology. If he insists on the lowly origin of ideas, he also believes that they can play a part in transfiguring the face of the earth.

* * *

The early Marx is engaged on an arrestingly original project. No other critic of the system under which he lived had taken it to task for what it does to the human senses. There had been no such phenomenology of capitalism before. In Marx's view, the capitalist mode of production comes under the sway of a supremely bodiless form of reason, one that assumes a variety of forms. 'All the physical and intellectual senses,' Marx comments in his *Economic and Philosophical Manuscripts*, 'have been replaced by the simple estrangement of all these senses – the sense of *having*. So that it might give birth to its inner wealth, human nature has been reduced to this absolute poverty.'[20] If acquisitiveness breeds abstraction, so, ironically, does poverty. The goods that the poor need in order to survive are stripped of their sensuous properties and reduced to what Marx calls an 'abstract form'. You do not care what you eat if you are starving, or what kind of work you can obtain if the alternative is to go hungry.

True human activity, by contrast, is a question of praxis – of the free realisation of one's sensory and spiritual powers as enjoyable ends in themselves. Its model for Marx is the work of art. It is a question of happiness or well-being, which for Marx as for Aristotle is an activity rather than a state of mind. The most authentic form of production or 'life activity' (notions which for Marx extend far beyond the factory floor) is one executed for its own sake, free from the goad of physical necessity; and this in his view is one vital distinction between human beings and their more utilitarian-minded fellow animals. Under capitalist conditions, however, 'life activity, productive life appears to man only as a means for the satisfaction of a need, the need to preserve physical existence'.[21] We work in order to live, not as a form of service, solidarity and self-fulfilment. At the same time, other men and women (what Marx describes as 'one's greatest wealth') become no more than a means for achieving one's ends, and are consequently dematerialised.

Capitalists are concerned with the products they churn out only in so far as they represent a means of reaping profit. Viewed as commodities rather than objects, they are pure abstractions, without a particle of materiality in their make-up. At the same time, the body of the producer is reduced to the status of a labouring instrument. He becomes a 'being with neither needs nor senses . . . and from being a man becomes an abstract activity and a stomach'.[22] In relieving others of their bodily wealth, however, capitalists lay violent hands on their own sensuous powers as well. Marx comments:

Self-denial, the denial of life and of all human needs is [bourgeois political economy's] principal doctrine. The less you eat, drink, buy books, go to the theatre, go dancing, go drinking, think, love, theorize, sing, paint, fence etc., the more you save and the greater will become that treasure which neither moths nor maggots can consume – your *capital*. The less you *are*, the less you give expression to your life, the more you *have*, the greater is your *alienated* life and the more you store up of your estranged life.[23]

Asceticism is the other face of acquisitiveness. Your capital becomes a vampiric power sucking the substance from your body. Marx himself was not much inclined to dancing, book-buying or theatre-going, given that (as he once remarked of himself) nobody had ever written so much about money and had so little. He did, however, indulge in the odd pub crawl.

Having alienated their sensory life to the power of capital, however, the less ascetically minded kinds of capitalist can retrieve it again in vicarious guise. 'Everything which you are unable to do,' Marx writes, 'your money can do for you: it can eat, drink, go dancing, go to the theatre, it can appropriate art, learning, historical curiosities, political power, it can travel, it is capable of doing all these things for you; it can buy everything.'[24] Capital is a phantasmal body, a monstrous *doppelgänger* which stalks abroad as its masters sleep, mechanically consuming the pleasures they austerely forgo.

There is another way in which the body can be stripped of its substance. It is in the *Economic and Philosophical*

Manuscripts that Marx expounds his theory of alienation, in which men and women cease to recognise themselves in the material world they produce. The products of their activity, once appropriated by a system of private ownership, cease to be expressive of that labour, so that individuals become strangers to themselves. As Elaine Scarry observes, Marx assumes 'that the made world is the human being's body and that, having projected that body into the made world, men and women are themselves disembodied, spiritualised'.[25] Capitalism, Marx maintains, 'estranges man from his own body'.[26] Individuals' labour is now no part of their essential being, but lies within the command of others. It is felt as a form of drudgery external to their real self, rather as the flesh for Cartesian dualism is external to the spirit. The material world thus ceases to be a phenomenological sphere. It is no longer a humanised terrain on which men and women move easily and spontaneously, having incorporated it into their flesh, but a realm that has confiscated their energies and so appears more alive than they do. In ceasing to be the taken-for-granted context of their activities, it looms up as an anonymous power determining their destinies. Because human beings are also alienated from each other, the body in the corporate sense of the word disintegrates as well. Since material reality constitutes a bond between individuals, to lose touch with that reality is also for them to lose touch with each other.

One of the goals of socialism, then, is to return to the body its plundered powers, so that the senses may be allowed to come into their own. This happens rather less dramatically in poetry, which seeks to restore to language something of the sensuous fullness that abstraction and utility have stripped from it. Only by loosening the grip of these forces over human affairs can we come to relish our sensory powers as ends in themselves. Materialism in the common-or-garden sense of the word – an excessive regard for material goods – is hostile to materiality. If we need to rid ourselves of the current social order, it is among other things because we are unable to taste, smell and touch as keenly as we might:

> The supersession of private property is therefore the complete emancipation of all human senses and attributes; but it is this emancipation because these senses and attributes have become human, subjectively as well as objectively. The eye has become a human eye, just as its object has become a social, human object, made by man for man. The senses have therefore become theoreticians in their immediate praxis. They relate to the thing for its own sake, but the thing itself is an objective human relation to itself and to man ... Need or enjoyment have therefore lost their egoistic nature, and nature has lost its mere utility in the sense that its use has become human use.[27]

In an astonishingly bold move, Marx argues his way up from the sentient body to ethics and politics – from what it is like to smell a chrysanthemum or listen to a sonata to the accumulation of capital, social relations, private property, ideology and the state. It will be left to Sigmund Freud to cast doubt on this euphoric vision of a human body benignly restored to itself. The body with which Marx deals would seem free of desire; and desire for Freud is a force that hollows and fragments the flesh. It, too, is a virulent form of abstraction, indifferent to the sensory features of things. Instead, we ransack the objects around us in search of some perpetually elusive reality at their core. It is not certain that this chronic disenchantment will find its cure in communism. There is a vacuity at the heart of the Freudian body which twists it out of true and sends its actions awry. The act of realising the self is always overshadowed by a residue that resists articulation.

Marxism is among other things an account of how the human body, through those prostheses known as culture and technology, comes to ensnare itself in its own powers and overreach itself. The tale it has to tell is thus a modern version of what the ancient Greeks knew as hubris. The world we invent spins out of our control and reduces us to its hirelings. Yet this does not come about simply because we are productive beings. For Marx, it is the result of the social relations in which our productive powers are caught up. And this is the point at which his somatic or anthropological materialism passes over into historical materialism. We now shift from describing how it is with the human animal to recounting a narrative about it. As long as our productive powers are fairly meagre, so the story goes, everyone has to labour simply to stay alive. Once society begins to generate an economic surplus, however, some individuals can be set free from the need to toil, and the result of this is the growth of social classes. A minority is able to seize control of production, dispose of the labour-power of others and appropriate for itself an inordinate slice of the surplus, while the majority battles to retain what it can of the fruits of its labour. Class struggle has set in. At the same time, a number of figures emerge – priests, bards, shamans, counsellors, medicine men and the like – who hold sway over what one might call spiritual production. Their modern heirs are known as the intelligentsia. One function of this intellectual coterie is to come up with ideas that lend credence to the status quo, a process to which Marx gives the name of ideology. There is also the need for a coercive power that will regulate class struggle in the interests of the exploiters. This is known as the state.

Social classes, then, emerge when the productive forces evolve to a certain point – one which is neither low enough to force everyone to work, nor high enough to permit everyone a sufficiency of goods without unpleasant exertion. The name of this latter state of affairs is communism. The only good reason for being a socialist, apart from annoying people you find disagreeable, is that you don't like having to work. Once there is enough of a surplus to be equitably shared, there is no more foundation for social classes, and consequently no more need for ideology or the state. In this sense, Marx's politics have a material foundation. Socialism cannot happen anywhere, any time. It is not just a good idea one might dream up at two o'clock in the morning, like distributing bank notes with a maniacal grin to bemused strangers on the street. It requires certain material preconditions; and if you try to achieve it without due attention to this fact, you are likely to end up with some form of Stalinism. This is one sense in which a materialist perspective has political implications.

There is, of course, a good deal more to historical materialism than this bare sketch would suggest. It is also the story of how one mode of production is transformed into another by political revolution, and how all this helps to mould the ideas by which we live. This last point is of some importance. The material conditions for, say, writing a novel include having a supply of food, some sort of writing instrument, enough health and sanity to sit at a desk and produce reasonably coherent sentences, a lock on your children's bedroom door, and so on; but it does not follow that the novel you produce somehow reflects these conditions. Marxist theory, by contrast, traces the imprint of our material needs and capabilities on supposedly much grander stuff: art, law, ethics, politics, philosophical systems and so on. In this sense, the material is not just what one starts from. Rather than being simply a necessary condition of one's activities, it shapes their character from beginning to end.

All the same, there is a sense in which the whole point of Marxism is to achieve a degree of independence from material forces. As long as we produce simply out of necessity, prodded into action by scarcity or animal need, we are not at our finest as a species. It is when we can attain a degree of distance from such wants, producing not only to satisfy them but also to exercise our creative powers, that we are at our most impressive. The irony, as we have seen already, is that this distance from the material is itself possible only under certain material conditions. We need such conditions in order to get beyond them. Something similar applies to human relationships. As long as social relations are largely determined by need and utility, we are unable to delight in each other's existence for its own sake. To do so, we need to be free from the largely instrumental treatment of others which class-society forces upon us; and this, too, ultimately depends on an increase in material resources. In a moving passage, Marx notes that this is possible even in the toil-stained present:

When communist workmen gather together, their immediate aim is instruction, propaganda, etc. But at the same

84

they acquire a new need – a need for society – and what appears as a means has become an end ... Smoking, eating and drinking, etc., are no longer means of creating links between people. Company, association, conversation, which in turn has society as its goal, is enough for them. The brotherhood of man is not a hollow phrase, it is a reality, and the nobility of man shines forth upon us from their work-worn figures.[28]

* * *

'Social being is not determined by consciousness,' Marx declares in *The German Ideology*, 'but consciousness by social being.'[29] The claim is a trap to catch the unwary. How can social being determine consciousness when consciousness is an integral part of it? Meanings, values, judgements, intentions and interpretations are not separate from social activity. On the contrary, there could be no such activity without them. To give a purely physical description of a lovers' quarrel is not to give a description of a lovers' quarrel. Human actions are *projects*, purposive forms of practice which forge a link between some current situation and a goal that lies beyond it. And you cannot have meaningless projects, unless by 'meaningless' you mean 'futile'. Hurling yourself through a plate glass window after a hard night on the town is meaningless in one sense but not in another.

In what sense, then, can social being be said to hold sway over consciousness? This is clearly true of individual men and women, who come to consciousness by sharing in a practical form of life. But in what sense is it true more generally? Marx has two responses to this question. For one thing, it is material need that compels us to produce, and such needs are not primarily a matter of consciousness. Such needs, to be sure, must become aware of themselves if they are to be satisfied. In this sense, thinking is a material necessity. But they germinate in the body rather than the mind. 'The need is what we think from', remarks Theodor Adorno in *Negative Dialectics*.[30] Something similar is true for Freud, in whose view the small infant is in the grip of an anarchic set of bodily drives from which the ego is yet to emerge. The mind is belated in relation to the body. When it does appear on the scene, it represses a good many of the forces which went into its making, thrusting them into that non-place we know as the unconscious.

For another thing, there is an ambiguity here about the term 'consciousness'. It can mean the ideas implicit in our everyday activity, or it can refer to formal systems of concepts such as law, art, politics, ideology and the like. All of this is what Marx calls the superstructure; and in his view, consciousness in this sense is indeed finally determined by the 'base', by which he means the social relations of production. The relations between base and superstructure, however, are not equivalent to those between action and thought. The former is a sociological affair, while the latter is an epistemological question. Thought is internal to action, the conceptual lining to its material sleeve, so to speak. But though there will be social relations of production in a future socialist order, Marx does not envisage the continuing existence of a superstructure. This is not to say that there would be no art, law or politics under communism, simply that these activities would no longer be called upon to legitimate the power of a ruling class.

It is a mistake to think of the relation between superstructure and base as one between consciousness and reality. It is rather a relation between different sets of social institutions. Superstructural set-ups like nightclubs, law courts, parliaments, museums, publishing houses and the like are quite as material as fishing vessels or canning factories. As with canning beans or fishing for herring, they consist of projects in which thought and action are inseparable. 'Superstructural' describes how ideas or activities function in relation to the material basis of social existence. It does not imply that we act first and think later.

If Marxism sees ideas as grounded in material history, then this doctrine must also apply to itself. It must be able to provide a historical analysis of its own origins. Historical materialism must subject itself to a materialist critique. In fact, Marxism goes one step further than giving an account of how such thought came into existence. It also sketches the material conditions under which it might pass out of existence again. Marx himself is clear that there is nothing timeless about his own beliefs. On the contrary, the sooner his ideas can be thrust into historical oblivion, the better. Philosophy is an activity whose primary aim is its own abolition. This is not the view of most practitioners of the trade. It is hard to imagine Plato or Kant eagerly anticipating a time when their work will be consigned to the garbage can. But this is just what Marx himself hopes of the future. He would doubtless have been dismayed to learn that his ideas were still alive, if not exactly kicking, in the twenty-first century. The fact that they were still in business could only mean that they had not been realised in practice. Once that had come about, Marxism itself could wither away. It is a strictly temporary affair, unlike being a Jew or a haemophiliac. In realising itself, Marxist theory also aims to eliminate itself. There would be no call for emancipatory theory in an emancipated society. The task of such theory is to help bring such a situation to birth, not to hang around in hope of further employment.

In scrutinising historical practices, philosophy tends to forget that it is one of them itself. Indeed, John Macmurray argues that 'the philosophy of any historical period reflects the life of the period even more evidently than does its art'.[31] Nietzsche scoffs:

You ask me about the idiosyncrasies of philosophers? There is their lack of historical sense, their hatred of even the idea of becoming . . . They think they are doing a thing *honour* when they dehistoricise it . . . when they make a mummy of it. All that philosophers have handled for millennia has been conceptual mummies; nothing actual has escaped from their hands alive.[32]

Marx, by contrast, is aware that his own ideas would not have been possible in the age of Chaucer, any more than Shakespeare could have stumbled across the Second Law of Thermodynamics. Marxism steps onto the historical stage only when it is both possible and necessary for it to do so – when, for example, history has evolved to the point where the categories Marxism employs (abstract labour, commodities, surplus value and so on) have become available in reality, and where to employ them is thought necessary for human emancipation. For socialist politics to get off the ground, a suitable instrument of that emancipation also needs to have emerged, which for Marx is the working class.

The fact that philosophy does not generally pay much heed to its own social context is one reason why it is not among Marx's favourite pursuits. Like Nietzsche and Wittgenstein, he is a supremely original philosopher with little faith in philosophy. In fact, one of his works is entitled *The Poverty of Philosophy*. The term 'materialist philosophy' might well have struck him as a contradiction in terms, since he sometimes argues as though philosophy is an endemically idealist pursuit. If he really did think this, he was clearly mistaken. It is hard to see how he could have done so, however, since he was well aware of the work of empiricist or materialist philosophers such as Francis Bacon, whose work he praised, not to speak of the radical *philosophes* of the French Enlightenment. It is rather that the current of philosophy he himself had to confront in Germany was mostly of an idealist kind, a fact which might occasionally have tempted him to mistake it for philosophy as such.

For the most part, Marx engages with this idealist world-view only to unmask it as a set of pseudo-problems, chimeras which would vanish were the material conditions that produce them to be transformed. This might well be the case with some conceptual puzzles. There are plenty of questions over which philosophers have agonised in the past which we have not so much resolved as dismissed as irrelevant. Nobody has come up with a satisfactory solution to the question of how many angels can dance on the head of a pin, not because it is beyond our mental capabilities but because we have better things to do. But this is not the same as putting paid to philosophy as such. It is doubtful that political revolution would resolve such questions as the nature of time or the foundations of morality, or make it abundantly clear why there is anything at all rather than nothing. Marx's own 'somatic' philosophy is unlikely to be superannuated by socialism. Besides, if thinking can be a pleasure, why should we wish to see the back of it?

Marx's attitude to philosophy is strikingly similar to Wittgenstein's. Both men believe that it is essential only when things have gone awry. Our relation to the world, Marx insists, is not in general a theoretical one; but there are times when we need to indulge in this abnormal form of discourse, if only to arrive at the point where we can throw it away. There is, however, an important difference between the two thinkers here. Marx is intent on clearing the philosophical ground in order to launch a theory (historical materialism) of his own, whereas Wittgenstein looks askance on all such theorising, a term he tends to use pejoratively. Even so, both authors are deeply sceptical of the view that thought is an autonomous activity. Philosophy tends to locate the origin of ideas in previous ideas. On the whole, it does not regard intellectual activity as bound up with practical existence. Indeed, to the popular mind, philosophy is the opposite of practice. 'He was philosophical about it' means that he concluded there was nothing he could do.

This attitude is scarcely surprising, given that philosophers are not in general the most practical of people. Plato takes a dim view of manual labour, even though his own writings would not have been possible without it. Every work of philosophy presupposes an invisible army of builders, plumbers, clothes manufacturers, farmers, truck drivers, lumberjacks, printers and so on. In Walter Benjamin's phrase, these men and women deal in 'the crude and material things without which no refined and spiritual things could exist'.[33] The story is told of a small boy, the son of an Oxford philosopher, who was showing a visitor around his father's study. 'See all those books?' he said proudly, waving to a bookcase filled with his father's works. 'My mother typed all those.' It is not surprising, then, that philosophers have had a problem about how the soul hooks up with the body. It is also unsurprising that those who spend their time contemplating the world from a leisurely distance might come to harbour doubts as to its existence. To some extent, philosophical idealism projects the philosopher's own situation onto the world at large and, being in this sense the result of specific material conditions, threatens to discredit its own belief in the sovereignty of mind.

For Marx, however, it is not just a question of the impracticality of professors. The illusion that thought stands free of material reality springs from the division between mental and manual labour, which can only arise at a certain stage of social evolution. Once the production of an economic surplus allows an intelligentsia to appear, he writes,

from this moment onwards consciousness can really flatter itself that it is something other than consciousness of existing practice, that it really represents something without representing something real; from now on consciousness is in a position to emancipate itself from the world and to proceed to the formation of 'pure' theory, theology, philosophy, ethics, etc.[34]

Ironically, then, the conviction that consciousness is a zone divorced from material existence has a sound material foundation. The gap between ideas and reality is itself a product of reality. Ideas and practical existence are related in such a way as to be divided. And this division has material consequences. Ideas cease to be what Marx calls 'a material force' for social change. Instead, they play a partisan role in society in their very aloofness from such ends. What looks like a non-relation between thought and reality is thus one way in which the two are most closely coupled.

'The same spirit that builds philosophical systems in the brain of the philosopher,' Marx writes, 'builds railways with the hands of the workman. Philosophy does not stand outside the world any more than man's brain is outside him because it is not his stomach . . . the head, too, belongs to the world.'[35] It is on account of such sentiments that he has been called 'perhaps . . . the greatest anti-philosopher of the modern age'.[36] Anti-philosophers are thinkers who come up with ideas that are suspicious of ideas (Marx, Nietzsche, Freud), or who are sceptical of a whole received style of philosophising (Derrida), or who are in grave doubt as to the value of philosophy as such (Marx, Wittgenstein). There are carnivalesque anti-philosophers who see it as their task to puncture thought's portentous self-importance, embarrassing it with the gross bulk of the body (Nietzsche, Mikhail Bakhtin). Nietzsche proclaims in *Ecce Homo* that he is not a philosopher but dynamite, a 'terrible explosive' whose conception of philosophy is worlds removed from that of the professors.[37] Thomas Aquinas dismissed his *Summa Theologica*, the most magnificent work of philosophical theology ever written, as so much 'straw'. Though he must have been aware that it was a masterpiece, he laid down his pen before it was complete, in what may well have been a deliberate act of humility.

Convinced that reason does not go all the way down, antiphilosophers delve beneath it to some more primordial reality: power, desire, difference, physiology, emotion, lived experience, religious faith, material interests, the life of the common people and so on. In the words of Ludwig Feuerbach, antiphilosophy attends to 'what in man does not philosophise, what is rather opposed to philosophy and abstract thought'.[38] Rather than dismiss philosophical talk, anti-philosophy seeks to reconstruct it through a vigilance to what it suppresses. About that of which philosophy must remain silent, it is necessary to speak.

In the pursuit of thinking otherwise, most of these authors are constrained to invent an alternative form of writing, one which questions the distinction between philosophy and literature (Kierkegaard, Nietzsche, Benjamin, Wittgenstein, Adorno, Cixous, Derrida). Since ethics, Wittgenstein argues, is a question of how to live rather than a theory or doctrine, it is art, not philosophy, that can most powerfully illuminate it. One turns for moral insight to Tolstoy and Dostoevsky, not to

Spinoza or Kant. He spoke of his later thought as representing a 'kink' in the history of philosophy similar to the invention of dynamics in science, and regards himself as an heir to the subject that used to be called philosophy.[39] 'Anti-philosophy,' declares Richard Rorty, 'is more unprofessional, funnier, more allusive, sexier, and above all more "written"' than conventional philosophy.[40] Wittgenstein, whose later literary style is splendidly companionable, held that philosophy should be written as a poetic composition, and dreamed of writing a philosophical work consisting entirely of jokes. (Since he was not the most waggish of individuals, it is perhaps just as well that this ambition was never realised.) Nietzsche, a superlative stylist, was a master of the aphorism who aspired to compress into ten sentences what everyone else took a book to spell out. True to his Surrealist interests, Walter Benjamin wanted to write a book consisting entirely of images.

Both Marx and Wittgenstein are alert to how ideas can become reified once ripped from their social contexts.[41] Marx comments in *The German Ideology*:

The philosophers would only have to dissolve their language into the ordinary language from which it is abstracted, to recognise it as the distorted language of the actual world, and to realise that neither thought nor language in themselves form a realm of their own, that they are only manifestations of actual life.[42]

95

If the claim could have sprung almost word for word from the pages of the later Wittgenstein, it may be because he was familiar with the text in which it occurs. *The German Ideology* was published in England in 1932, and Wittgenstein may have been handed a copy of it by one of his Marxist colleagues at Cambridge.

It is a situation in which ideas are wrenched from their contexts that we encounter in Thomas Hardy's novel *Jude the Obscure*, the epigraph of which reads 'The letter killeth'. The work portrays a late-Victorian England full of idols, myths, phantoms and efficacious illusions, thronged with fetishists and ghost-seers. It is a necrophiliac social order in love with death, in which the fortunes of the living fall under the despotic sway of dead creeds. The novel sees in its own way that capitalism is both grossly materialistic and spookily dematerialising, at once too carnal and too ethereal. Marx finds just the same ambiguity in the commodity form.

One word for an efficacious illusion is a novel. Hardy, in his preface to the first edition, describes *Jude* as dramatising 'a deadly war between flesh and spirit', by which he means a social order whose material institutions thwart human freedom. If it is a materialist work, it is among other things because it rejects this social version of mind–body dualism, and it does so by pointing to two forms of human activity which promise to resolve it. One of them is art – more precisely, the craftsmanship by which Jude Fawley, a stonemason, earns his living repairing the crumbling colleges of the University of Oxford. To carve stone is to invest a chunk of matter with meaning, converting it into a signifier of spirit. Jude spends his time reinforcing the walls of the very colleges that shut him out, refusing to admit him as an undergraduate; but the novel is clear enough that this form of labour is more precious than the lucubrations of the dons.

The other activity that promises to transcend the dualism of flesh and spirit is sexual love. In the relationship between Jude and Sue Bridehead, a mutuality of bodies becomes the occasion for a reciprocity of selves, as the flesh grows eloquent and expressive. It is not, however, a sexual equality that Victorian England finds easy to accommodate, which is why in *Jude* it steps in to break up the relationship, kill off the protagonist and drive his partner into guilty self-loathing. Sexual repression is not a subject with which Marx concerned himself. There is no doubt, however, that he would have recognised in Jude's craftsmanship an image of non-alienated labour, for all the dispiriting conditions in which it is performed. What we know as craft mediates between the self-delight of art and the practicality of labour; and it is to such images of production that Marx looks in his pursuit of a social order which might welcome the Fawleys of this world rather than cast them out.

CHAPTER FOUR

High Spirits

MARX AND NIETZSCHE form such a political contrast that it is easy to overlook how much they have in common. Both are materialists for whom the noble has its origins in the base. Both view knowledge as essentially practical, grounding it in the body. For Marx, knowledge in class-society is largely in the service of power, while for Nietzsche it fulfils that role at all times and in all places. Indeed, power is a central motif for them both, though Nietzsche regards it as the ultimate reality, while Marx holds to something more fundamental still, namely the material interests which power protects or contests. He might well have dismissed Nietzsche's exuberant vision of the world as will to power – as a place where every material body strives to grow and flourish by exercising dominion over others – as a kind of cosmic capitalism. 'Life itself,' Nietzsche writes, 'is *essentially* appropriation, injury, overpowering of what is alien and weaker; suppression, hardness, imposition of one's own forms, incorporation and at least, at its mildest, exploitation.'[1] To the pious bourgeois who throws up his hands in horror at this vision, Nietzsche's response is: look at the beliefs inherent in your own everyday behaviour. Look at what you do in your counting house, not at what you intone in church.

Both men are wary of the consolations of idealism. Both see false consciousness as afflicting the great mass of humanity – temporarily so for Marx, permanently so for Nietzsche. In their resolute this-worldliness, they reject all metaphysical fictions and bogus spirituality. Both suspect altruism and humanitarianism of cloaking the harsh realities of exploitation. They are also, in Nietzsche's word, 'immoralists', refusing to treat morality as an autonomous sphere of its own and insisting on its role in a broader material history. That they are historicists is another of their affinities. Nietzsche may not be a historical materialist, but his thought is both historical and materialist. The two authors' views of history are also in some ways parallel. By and large, the human saga has been for both men a bloodstained narrative of violence, conflict and oppression – though Marx discerns an intelligible pattern in this tale, while Nietzsche calls it 'a gruesome dominion of nonsense and accident'.[2]

For Marx, we can advance into the future only by recollecting the trauma of the past; for Nietzsche, we can march forward only by a kind of heroically willed amnesia. Both thinkers, however, are convinced that the wretched history of humankind can be overcome – for Marx by communism, for Nietzsche by the advent of the Overman (*Übermensch*). In both cases, the seeds of this transcendence are already being sown – and sown, ironically, in the very misfortunes of the present. What Nietzsche calls the moral era is the chronicle of humanity's self-torment and self-loathing; yet by refining and spiritualising human beings, this cheerless condition lays the ground for a choice few of them to become as gods. Marx has a more universal redemption in his sights; but it, too, will come about through adversity– in his case, by the wretched of the earth coming to power.

For both men, then, victory is plucked from weakness. Humanity in Nietzsche's eyes is 'more sick, uncertain, change-able, indeterminate than any other animal',[3] yet it is pregnant with a glorious future. Both philosophers sing the praises of civilisation while conscious of the frightful price it has exacted from humanity – what Theodor Adorno calls 'the horror teeming under the stone of culture'.[4] Every advance in history has been paid for in the coinage of subjugation, every small step in civility attained through spiritual and physical torture. In this conviction, both Marx and Nietzsche are close to the thought of Sigmund Freud, for whom civilisation may well demand from men and women a sacrifice too painful to be worth enduring. Indeed, all three men can be seen as tragic thinkers – not because they despair of a less dreary future, but because that future can be secured only on the basis of a history which is terrible beyond words. It is the tragic spirit, uniquely, which is able to stare this horror in the face yet still affirm.

There are other points of contact between Marx the champion of the plebs and Nietzsche the scourge of them. If Marx spurns religion as so much ideology, Nietzsche produces what is perhaps the most magnificent polemic against its crimes and follies that the modern age has witnessed. Both men embrace a Romantic ethics of self-realisation, for which the good life consists in the free expression of one's powers as an end in itself. Both find a model of this creativity in art, which is Nietzsche's theme from beginning to end.[5] There are differences all the same. For Marx, as we have seen, self-realisation must be a reciprocal affair, whereas Nietzsche's haughty Overman stands in contemptuous solitude, disdainful of human sympathy and solidarity. The idea of equality is an affront to his sense of the unique specificity of things, the utter incommensurability of one phenomenon with another. For him, even to say 'leaf' or 'waterfall' is to falsify. Yet Marx, too, rejects what one might call an exchange-value of the spirit, dismissing any abstract conception of equality as bourgeois rather than socialist.

Nietzsche is an astonishingly adventurous thinker. Philosophically speaking, he is far more radical than Marx. He casts doubt on truth, fact, objectivity, logic, objects, subjects, agents, souls, natures, will, law, science, progress, virtue, causality, necessity, substance, purpose, unity, attribute, being, ego, identity, species, materiality, conscience and duration, along with a number of other received ideas. This doesn't leave a lot still standing. He rejects the ethics and epistemology of middle-class society, scorns its sentimental idealism, shatters its scientific totems and supernatural comforts and kicks out the foundations from under all social order and political stability. He is in truth every bit as dangerous a thinker as he flatters himself as being.

Politically speaking, Nietzsche is quite as radical as Marx, once one recalls that radicalism is by no means the monopoly of the left. If one is to take him at his word, he looks forward to a future of global warfare in which there will be a reversion to slavery, the poor will be prevented from breeding and weaker peoples will be crushed or even exterminated. 'The weak and ill-constituted shall perish', he announces in *The Anti-Christ*,[6] though whether they will wither away of their own accord, or with a little help from the likes of Nietzsche himself, is not clear. The brutality of his politics is in marked contrast to the subtlety of his thought. As a sworn enemy of peace, compassion, democracy, effeminacy, independent women and the proletarian rabble, he is in love with everything cruel, severe, wicked, manly, malicious, vindictive and domineering. Love of one's neighbour is despicable, and pity runs contrary to the law of evolution. It is the sick, not the evil, who are a source of spiritual danger. There is a deadly line of descent from the New Testament, a document which Nietzsche comically accuses of lacking good breeding, to the debacle of the French Revolution and from there to the most detestable *canaille* of all, the socialists who teach envy and resentment to working men meekly content with their lot. A fear of the terrible vengeance of the masses runs as a steady subtext throughout his work, composed as it is in the shadow of the Paris Commune.

Unlike Marx, then, Nietzsche would not make the ideal companion for a pub crawl. All one can plead in his defence is that he loathed German nationalism and voiced his contempt for anti-Semites, while making a fair number of anti-Semitic comments himself. He was also quite as pitiless a critic of orthodox society as Marx, though from the far right rather than the revolutionary left. When it comes to Nietzsche, that left must grapple with a thinker who shares its own historicist and materialist bent, its aversion to metaphysical myths and sentimental moralism, while apparently eager to grind the faces of the poor even deeper in the dust. Most post-structuralist readings of Nietzsche avoid this dilemma by the simple device of suppressing his politics.

Like Marx, Nietzsche is a somatic materialist. 'Soul,' he declares in *Thus Spake Zarathustra*, 'is only a word for some-thing about the body.' (Surprisingly for one who preferred watching westerns to reading philosophy, Wittgenstein appears to have been familiar with this statement. The work of Nietzsche was by no means unknown to him. 'Am I saying something like, "and the soul itself is merely something about the body"?' he asks himself. 'No. (I am not that hard up for categories.)'⁷ His point, however, is that the concept of soul plays a legitimate part in our language games, not that soul and body are existentially separate. 'You say "I",' Nietzsche goes on, 'and are proud of this word. But greater than this – although you will not believe it – is your body and its great intelligence, which does not say "I" but performs "I".'⁸

The body has its wisdom, then, of which the mind knows nothing. It is a richer, more astonishing phenomenon than consciousness, which for Nietzsche is shallow, generalising, falsifying, rather stupid stuff. The concept of soul, he claims, was invented to denigrate the body and make it appear diseased. It first emerges when our robust animal instincts are thwarted and forced back on themselves, creating an inner space in which they fester and grow morbid. In this sense, subjectivity itself is a form of sickness. So-called spirit is a Hamlet-like virus which infects our vital instincts and causes them to falter. It is an imperfection of the organism, a glitch in our spontaneous activity. The soul can also be seen as a 'grammatical habit', a ruse of language by which are tricked into positing a subject to account for whatever takes place. It is a Wittgensteinian kind of argument, as we shall see later.

Nietzsche himself will no longer 'trace the origin of man in the "spirit", in "divinity"; we have placed him back among the animals'.[9] He asks himself in *The Gay Science* whether philosophy has 'not been merely an interpretation of the body and a *misunderstanding of the body*', and regards it as the great blind spot of all traditional thought. 'Philosophy says away with the *body*, this wretched *idée fixe* of the senses, infected with all the faults of logic that exist, refuted, even impossible, although it be imprudent enough to pose as if it were real!'[10] He himself will extend a friendly hand to this philosophical pariah and try to think history, culture, art and reason through again in terms of its appetites and aversions. 'It is our needs that interpret the world', he remarks in *The Will to Power*.[11] The body in his view is an open, malleable phenomenon with no fixed boundaries, continually assimilating alien stuff into its substance in the process of mastering its environment.

Consciousness, which Nietzsche sees in Marxian mode as having 'evolved through social intercourse and with a view to the interests of social intercourse',[12] has been absurdly over-valued. To think is to reduce the complexity of the world to the crudest sketch. A thinker, he scoffs, is one who simplifies. Language is consciousness in action, just as it is for Marx, but in Nietzsche's view it fatally dilutes the density of experience. Truth, too, has been inflated in importance. There are circumstances in which a fruitful falsehood may well prove preferable to it. It is simply an instrument of the drive to preserve and enhance human life, which Nietzsche calls will to power. 'Knowing that' is a function of 'knowing how', a claim that we also find in the work of Wittgenstein.

For Nietzsche as for Freud, the mind is a product of the bodily drives. It is those 'psycho-physiologists' or philosophers of the future like Nietzsche himself who are able to hear the enigmatic murmurings of the body in what others regard as a purely mental realm. Physiology must now become the starting point. While Kant posits a special faculty to account for the unity of our perceptions, Nietzsche regards such unity as the work of the body itself. The whole of our conscious life is in the service of our basic animal functions, and philosophy is the name we give to the style of thought that suppresses this humiliating truth. At first glance, the body would seem the most solid, self-evident fact about human beings, but it is actually a dark continent quite impenetrable to thought. Since we cannot be aware of the myriad impulses that make up any one of our thoughts or actions, we are profoundly inexplicable to ourselves. The deepest mystery is thus the one most palpably to hand. Consciousness, Nietzsche writes in *Daybreak*, is 'a more or less fantastic commentary' on a text (the body) which is unknown and perhaps unknowable.[13]

Nietzsche's somatic materialism has its more ludicrous aspects. Genuine thought, he considers, requires fresh air, good weather and a healthy diet, along with 'undemanding and obedient intestines, busy as windmills yet distant'.[14] It is not clear whether this is what he means by calling himself a 'terrible explosive'. There is a good deal of the Boy Scout syndrome in his work. With his love of solitary walks in high mountains, his comically self-idealising talk of undertaking 'dangerous journeys of exploration and spiritualised North Pole expeditions under desolate and dangerous skies',[15] Nietzsche is too often to be found mistaking philosophising for a cold shower. With solemn absurdity, he notes that the will is stronger in the north of Germany than in the centre, that all prejudices arise from the intestines, and that the ancient Celts were blond and not dark. Whereas most of his postmodern admirers are churlishly sceptical of science, Nietzsche himself relishes what he regards as its hard, cool, clean, rigorous, masculine spirit, in contrast to the feminine sogginess of religion and idealism. There are times when it is hard to say whether he is a philosopher or a personal trainer. He philosophises with his nose: 'The "entrails" of every soul,' he boasts, 'are physiologically perceived by me – *smelled*.'[16] All contact between individuals, he warns, involves some degree of uncleanness, and the turgidity of German thought has much to do with poor digestion. It is tempting to turn this vulgar materialism back on Nietzsche himself and ask whether his obsession with power and high spirits springs from his own chronic ill-health. Do we owe the idea of the Overman to the fact that he contracted syphilis as a student?

Morality and philosophy are in Nietzsche's eyes simply a kind of sign-language of the instincts and affects. One must read these phenomena symptomatically, grasping their claims as driven by envy, aggression, aversion, vengeance, anxiety and so on. All our perceptions contain an ineradicable element of fear, fantasy, ignorance, prejudice, self-aggrandisement and the like. Philosophy, he comments, is 'most often desire of the heart that has been filtered and made abstract'.[17] It is our affects, not our intellects, that interpret the world. A number of examples may serve to illustrate the point. Nihilism, anarchism and the Judaeo-Christian contempt for the senses stem from a loss of racial or national vigour, a corruption and impoverishment of human powers. It was degenerate blood consequent on widespread disease after the Thirty Years' War that laid the ground for the servility of modern German thought. Christianity and democracy represent the crafty victory of the weak over the strong, infecting noble spirits with their own loathsome subservience. Scepticism springs from the decline and nervous exhaustion of a race or class. The philosophers' vision of a world of stable objects, well-founded truths and inherent meanings reflects not their insight but their anxiety. The strongest will is one that can dispense with the myth of inherent meaning. Those who do not know how to put their will into things put meaning into them instead. If the study of causality is gratifying, it is because to trace phenomena to their origins is to gain power over them. The same applies to knowledge in general. If moral philosophers claim that the will is free, it is so that they can hold men and women responsible for their actions and punish them for their transgressions. Nietzsche even detects a plebeian hostility to privilege in the concept of physical laws, which treat all bodies alike.

'Suppose nothing else were "given" as real except our world of desires and passions', Nietzsche muses in *Beyond Good and Evil*.[18] Even this is not the firm bedrock it sounds, since desires and passions, along with the body itself, are products of the will to power; and though the will to power is really all there is, it is no kind of sturdy foundation, simply a network of elusive, eternally shifting forces. If this is so, then it is worth noting that Nietzsche is a somatic materialist but not a metaphysical one. He does not believe that matter is all there is. In fact, he does not believe in matter at all. It is a fictional way of describing a world made up of dynamic quanta of force and their fleeting configurations. He is also an implacable foe of mechanical materialism, which in his view simply replaces God with a cult of matter. Nor is he an epistemological materialist. The mind does not conform to the way the world is because the world is no way in particular. It is in perpetual flux, and it is we who invest it with truth, order and meaning. If we seem to discover certain laws in Nature, it is because we have smuggled them into it ourselves. If the world appears logical, it is because we have logicised it. It is we who have projected cause, sequence, law, number, objects, subjects, motive, purpose, constraint, regularity and so on into the seething chaos of reality, only to proceed to submit ourselves like an idolater to the work of our own hands.

All this, in Nietzsche's view, is the function of reason – a deceitful old woman, as he calls it with his customary political correctness. Reason is a device for simplifying and regulating the rich complexity of things so that we may take possession of them. It is thus wholly in the service of the will to power, constructing a world in which our capacities might be enriched and enhanced. Truth is simply reality tamed and tabulated by our practical needs, made regular, calculable and to that extent falsified. It is a fiction we need in order to survive and flourish. Untruth is thus a condition of life. (This, one might claim, disqualifies Nietzsche from being a kosher pragmatist, since for the pragmatist truth just is what helps us to flourish, whereas for Nietzsche a falsehood can achieve this end as well.) In the struggle to establish a moral ideal, for example, 'how much reality has to be misunderstood and slandered, how many lies have to be sanctified, how many consciences disturbed?'[19] Reason dumbs reality down; and though this is essential for our survival, it is also an aspect of what Nietzsche witheringly calls 'herd consciousness'. The Overman, by contrast, does not argue his reasons, since dialectics belongs to the rabble. Instead, he issues commands.

Language reflects not how things are but what we make of them. Propositions have sense only within certain domains of discourse, certain species-related ways of dividing up the world; and these domains of discourse are in turn bound up with our material needs and drives.

This, as we shall see, is remarkably close to Wittgenstein's insistence on the relations between a language game and a practical form of life. What counts as an object for Nietzsche is determined by the rules and concepts of a grammar whose foundation is ultimately anthropological. It is true that we sometimes feel ourselves running up against brute facts, but what we are actually doing, he insists, is ramming our heads against an interpretation of the world which has become so deeply embedded that we are currently unable to shake it off. The truth is that there are no facts, only interpretations. Whether this claim is itself a fact or an interpretation is not a question to which Nietzsche provides an answer.

* * *

Nietzsche does not believe in giving free rein to one's instincts. He is no Romantic libertarian in the style of D.H. Lawrence or Gilles Deleuze. The Overman is not a marauding barbarian but a courteous, cheerful, high-spirited, self-disciplined individual, rather as Nietzsche liked to see himself. Humanity has been degutted of its animal instincts, persuaded by the priests and philosophers to be ashamed of its senses, and reduced to the state of self-mutilation commonly known as virtue. The most it can aspire to is 'herd' behaviour. Yet this sorry condition, 'the most terrible sickness that has ever raged in man',[20] must be judged dialectically, as Marx approaches capitalism in much the same spirit. If it is the greatest disaster ever to befall humanity, it also tempers, refines and disciplines its drives, thus paving the way for the Overman who will incorporate his animal spirits into his reason, rather than using his reason to repress his instincts. Civilisation is a tale of barbarism, but without such brutality nothing precious would be produced.

Marx and Nietzsche are at one in this dialectical view. In Nietzsche's eyes, what the humanists and idealists fail to perceive is just 'how much blood and suffering lie at the root of all "good things"!'[21] Culture is the fruit of a calamitous history of crime, guilt, debt, torture, violence and exploitation. For his part, Marx holds that civilisation has only one progenitor – labour – and that socialism must be built on the proceeds of exploitation. In order to thrive, it demands an abundance of material and spiritual goods; and it inherits these resources from a history in which the business of accumulating them involves hardship and injustice. The prosperity which might one day lay the ground for freedom is itself the fruit of unfreedom.

There is, however, a key difference between the two thinkers on this score. Nietzsche has no doubt that bloodshed and suffering are fully justified if they result in the flourishing of superior types like himself. It is here that he parts company with Freud, who remarks in *The Future of an Illusion* that any civilisation in which the gratification of the few depends on the wretchedness of the many 'neither has nor deserves the prospect of a lasting existence'.[22] For Marx, the fact that barbarism has been an indispensable condition of civilisation is a tragic truth, whereas Nietzsche pens a celebrated study of tragedy which is among other things an attempt to justify this irony. In *The Birth of Tragedy*, the Dionysian stands among other things for the violence and destructiveness of existence, and the Apollonian for the sweetness and light of civilisation; but the opposition between them can be dismantled, since the Dionysian gives birth to the healing illusions of the Apollonian as a defence against its own rapaciousness. If we want visions of peace and harmony, then, it would appear that we need torment to inspire them. Bliss is born of pain, and beauty is a sublimation of suffering. It is a curiously perverse case, as though one were to claim that it is worth breaking your leg simply to savour the soothing effects of the anaesthetic.

In this sense, one can read Nietzsche's theory of tragedy as an allegory of his materialist theory of history. But it is also a form of theodicy, or justification of evil. Nietzsche regards slavery as a necessary condition of every vigorous culture, and warns his more egalitarian-minded compatriots that if one wants slaves it is foolish to educate them as masters. A vibrant aristocracy accepts with a good conscience 'the sacrifice of untold human beings who, *for its sake*, must be reduced and lowered to incomplete human beings, to slaves, to instruments'.[23] Whole races and classes may have to go under for higher types to prevail. In a passage excluded from *The Birth of Tragedy*, Nietzsche brazenly proposes that in modern times 'the misery of the laboriously living masses must be further intensified in order to enable a number of Olympian people to produce the world of art'.[24] The great majority of individuals, he announces in *The Will to Power*, have no right to existence, and are nothing but a misfortune to higher examples of the species.

What would Marx – who seems unaware of Nietzsche's work and who died before the publication of some of his most seminal writings – have made of his politics? He would, of course, have noted their squalor with some distaste. But there is more to be said than that. It would doubtless not have escaped his attention that *On the Genealogy of Morals* is a historical and materialist treatment of its subject, which was not only unusual for its time but represents a rare enough venture today. Just as unusually, the work is a class-analysis of morality, one which turns on the transition from an aristo-cratic ethics to the middle-class mores which come in its wake. In the early period of civilisation, when humanity needed to fight to survive, it was the values of a hardy, swash-buckling warrior class which proved most useful: conquest, cruelty, rivalry, rancour, vengeance, aggression and so on. Once civilisation was up and running, however, these values shed their social utility and came to be branded as evil, while the humanitarian virtues of peace, pity, meekness and compassion were held up instead for general admiration. Those who come to power in a Christian, democratic, spiritually gutless age are those whose instincts are feeble enough to be tamed – a spiritual castration to which they give the name of religion or morality. One can trace this transition in seventeenth-century England, though Nietzsche does not do so himself. In the middle of the century, Thomas Hobbes was still championing the aristocratic values of courage, honour, glory and greatness of soul; by the end of the century, John Locke was speaking up for the middle-class values of peace, tolerance and private property.

Since conquest, aggression and dominion are aspects of the will to power, and since the will to power is identical with all that is flourishing and robust, middle-class morality represents a betrayal of life itself. Even so, despite its meek, pacific character, bourgeois society continues to be in its own way every bit as aggressive and exploitative as the freebooting nobility which came before it, not least when it comes to its behaviour in the marketplace. It is simply that it is in denial about this truth. And the name of that denial is morality. The result is a grotesque discrepancy between how this social order sees itself in theory and what it actually gets up to in practice. What it proclaims is at odds with what it performs. It has killed off God, for example, since there is really no place for him in secular, materialistic society; but it is too craven to acknowledge its own act of deicide and continues to behave as though the absolute values which God represents are still in business. In a curious kind of cognitive dissonance, it does not believe in God, but it does not know that it doesn't. For Nietzsche to proclaim the death of God, then, is to demand that the stout burghers of his age confront the terrifying, exhilarating consequences of their own ultimate act of Oedipal revolt.[25]

Middle-class civilisation, then, lives by an ideology which fails to chime with what it actually does. And such ideologies, being thinly rooted in reality, are likely to prove ineffectual. Yet if the official world-view of the middle classes were to reflect what they get up to in reality, the result would be a set of values which were grounded in their practical activity but which failed to *legitimate* it. They would be incapable of presenting that practical activity in an appealing light. Ideally, your values should represent a sublimated version of what you actually do, so that they can both reflect and ratify it; but in marketplace conditions this is far from easy to achieve.

It is to this dilemma that Nietzsche's turn to a noble warrior class offers a convenient solution. For the outlook of that class reflects something of the incessant warring of the modern-day marketplace, but in doing so invests it with a glamour and grandeur of soul it lacks in reality. In fact, Nietzsche speaks at one point of the need for manufacturers to become noble. They would then be all the more successful in keeping the spectre of socialism at bay. His thought thus runs parallel to an English tradition of social thought, from Coleridge and Carlyle to Ruskin and Disraeli, which appeals to certain feudalist ideals (order, community, hierarchy, reverence, spiritual authority) as a solution to the ills of industrial capitalism.[26] By grafting a set of imported values onto the status quo, you can hope to lend it the spiritual legitimacy it has failed to generate for itself. The risk, however, is that the gap between those values and everyday life will then loom embarrassingly large.

The Overman may put the fear of God into timid bourgeois citizens, but he also heaves into view as their monstrous alter ego. His lordly way with law, stability and social consensus is bound to hold a secret allure to entrepreneurs, who must continually transgress boundaries themselves. In order to do so, however, they must depend on a stout framework of social order – on God, state, church, family, moral absolutes and metaphysical certitudes. Yet, if this order facilitates their activity, it also threatens to frustrate it. Nietzsche's solution to this problem is hair-raisingly radical. It is to sacrifice order to enterprise. Simply throw away frameworks and foundations so that human beings may live adventurously, experimentally, unleashing that infinite productivity which is will to power. Middle-class society was not misguided enough to accept this proposal. As a theory, it may enliven a philosophy seminar, but it is no way to stop the lower orders from getting out of hand.

'Life' is Nietzsche's highest value from start to finish, as it is the creed of one of his spiritual legatees, D.H. Lawrence. It is the life-deniers – a motley array of priests, pessimists, nihilists, Jews, Christians, Kantians, Darwinists, disciples of Socrates and Schopenhauer – for whom he reserves his most venomous polemic. But 'life' is a fatally vague concept. For Nietzsche, it means living in the overflowing abundance of one's creative powers; but who is to say what this involves, beyond riding roughshod over inferior life-forms? The agents in question might be thought the best judges; but does this mean that authentic life is whatever they declare it to be? And can they not be self-deceived? Does 'life' involve giving free rein to all of one's capabilities, however potentially devastating? That would be a naturalistic ethics with a vengeance. To live in the fullness of one's powers is in Nietzsche's eyes to live as the universe does, for it too, being nothing but will to power, continually extends and enhances itself. Yet why should living well mean conforming to the nature of the cosmos? Many a moralist has advocated just the opposite. And if the will to power extends and enhances itself in any case, what is so precious about acting in a way which plugs into this process?

Nietzsche opposes life to morality. In doing so, however, he fails to appreciate that the most resourceful moral thought, from Aristotle and Aquinas to Hegel and Marx, views morality precisely in terms of human flourishing. It recognises all the same that one needs to specify what counts as such flourishing in a given situation, which is what moral discourse serves to do; and on this question Nietzsche himself is mostly silent. He is unable to come up with the criteria by which one might judge an action to be an authentic flourish of life. (One such criterion – the general augmenting of human happiness – is a particular object of his derision. Only the Englishman, he jeers, believes that.) Marx, by contrast, has such a criterion, which he inherits from Hegel: morally commendable action involves realising one's powers reciprocally, in and through the similar self-realisation of others. It is not a knock-down argument. But it is an advance on claiming that enslaving entire peoples is justified by the fact that it yields you a gratifying sense of euphoria.

CHAPTER FIVE

The Rough Ground

'In the beginning was the deed', Ludwig Wittgenstein declares in *On Certainty*, quoting from Goethe's *Faust* and (though almost certainly without being aware of it) Leon Trotsky's *Literature and Revolution*. 'It is our *acting*,' he writes, 'that lies at the bottom of the language-game.'[1] It is, one might venture, Wittgenstein's own version of Marx's claim that social being determines consciousness. Our manifold ways of speaking are bound up with our practical forms of life, and make sense only within such a context. As A.C. Grayling comments, Wittgenstein means by a form of life 'the underlying consensus of linguistic and non-linguistic behaviour, assumptions, practices, traditions and natural propensities which humans, as social beings, share with one another, and which is therefore presupposed in the language they use'.[2] Alasdair MacIntyre remarks:

Uttering syntactically impeccable sentences at regular intervals is not exhibiting a capacity to use language . . . the use of a language is always embedded in forms of social practice and to understand adequately what is said on particular occasions in a given language one must have some at least of the abilities of a participant in the relevant form of social practice.[3]

Wittgenstein's case is more than the banal assertion that words can have powerful social implications. It suggests that we must look to the vast network of human practices, as well as to the natural bodily substratum which sustains them, in order to grasp the meaning of terms such as 'perhaps' and 'in', not just terms like 'liberty' and 'patriotism'. Corporeal beings like ourselves need the word 'perhaps' because we are subject to time, space, chance, error, incomplete knowledge, limited rational capabilities, ambiguous situations, the plurality and instability of the material world, the need to undertake complex, often unpredictable enterprises and so on. This is not the case with angels. Angels do not need the word 'perhaps' because they are not corporeal entities existing in a mutable material world, and are thus free of the contingencies that afflict human beings. Imperfect creatures like ourselves are bound to question our own assumptions from time to time, become in Nietzschean phrase 'philosophers of the dangerous "maybe" ',[4] but angels are subject to no such spasms of self-doubt. Nor do they need the word 'in', since in the absence of spatial relations they acknowledge no distinction between inner and outer – a distinction without which our own projects would grind to a halt. That humans use words like 'in' and 'perhaps' might tell an astute observer on Alpha Centauri quite a lot about them. It is in this sense that 'to imagine a language is to imagine a form of life', as Wittgenstein remarks in the *Philosophical Investigations*.[5]

It may seem strange, then, that in Wittgenstein's later thought this broadly materialist case goes hand-in-hand with an insistence that 'language remains self-contained and autonomous'.[6] Is not this the kind of view we associate with linguistic idealism – with, let's say, the theories of Wittgenstein's contemporary Ferdinand de Saussure, for whom language constitutes a closed semiotic system, one in which the sign stands free of what it refers to? How can the signifier be free-floating if language is woven into our practical existence? For Wittgenstein, however, these two claims are aspects of the same case. To assert that language is autonomous is not to doubt that it can come up from time to time with true or false statements about the world. What Wittgenstein is denying is that it does so by being somehow connected up with reality. On this theory, the word *kuccha* – which, as the reader will not need to be informed, means the short trousers worn as one of the five distinguishing signs of the Sikh Khalsa – acquires its meaning by being correlated with a pair of short trousers on a real-life Sikh. This, in Wittgenstein's view, is rather like imagining that the value of a coin is determined by the ham sandwich you buy with it, rather than by the coin's function in the economy as a whole.

Wittgenstein rejects this theory of meaning on a number of grounds, one of which is that it looks a lot less plausible when it comes to terms like 'nondescript', 'sneakily' or 'Oh, Christ'. It is a noun-centred theory of meaning, consistent with a thing-centred view of the world. 'You can't understand how words relate to things,' Charles Taylor points out, 'until you identify the nature of the activity in which they get related to things.'[7] In this spirit, Wittgenstein regards meaning as the way a word functions in a specific form of life. It is a social practice, not a state of mind or a ghostly correlation between signs and objects. As one commentator remarks, 'language, reason, meaning and mind are for Wittgenstein all forms of activity'.[8] Language does not 'reflect' reality or hook up with it; it is a material reality in itself. Our concepts, Wittgenstein comments in his *Remarks on Colour*, do not mirror our way of life but 'stand in the middle of it'.[9] And this is clearly more of a materialist than idealist standpoint.

Wittgenstein may see language as an autonomous activity, but he is not the sort of linguistic idealist one finds everywhere in a postmodern culture for whom it 'constructs' reality. Rather, it is men and women who construct it by their practical projects, and language is woven into this undertaking.

It is in our speaking that these forms of activity are sedimented. As Marx puts it, in eminently Wittgensteinian style, 'the production of ideas, of conceptions, of consciousness, is . . . directly interwoven with the material intercourse of men, the language of real life'.[10] What constitutes an object for human beings is not language, but the social activities which language crystallises. Truth and falsehood are linguistic affairs; but if they are not 'just' linguistic, it is because language is not just linguistic either. It is bound up with everyday practices; and those practices, as we shall see later, are in turn grounded in the nature of the human body. Language is always more than language. To have access to it is to have access to a world. It is what opens up reality, not what cuts us off from it.

What Wittgenstein calls a 'grammar' is a set of rules by which we are able to make sense of things; and such grammars are not correlated with reality. It is not as though some of them provide us with a more accurate representation of the world than others, as some utterances may be said to do. That would be like claiming that Polish captures the nature of things more faithfully than Urdu, or that placing the verb at the end of a sentence is more correct than placing it somewhere in the middle. One is reminded of the English patriot who claimed that English was the most natural language of all, since the words occur in the order in which you think them. Grammars are what allow us to use terms like 'accurate', 'representation' and 'correct' meaningfully in the first place. One grammar may be more useful than another, and all of them generate propositions which can be judged true or false; but they themselves are anterior to truth, and autonomous of the world in something like the sense that the rules of a game are autonomous. The rules of chess do not 'reflect' the way the game is; they are what constitute it as a game in the first place. We could always dream up another set of rules by which the pieces would move in entirely different ways. Reality for Wittgenstein does not instruct us in how to go about dividing it up, any more than it does for Nietzsche.

In Wittgenstein's view, however, this does not mean that we can carve reality up in any way we wish. We alter our concepts, he claims in *Zettel*, when we discover new facts. It is not a claim likely to warm the heart of the linguistic idealists, for whom facts are simply interpretations that happen to have caught on. This is why they feel an irresistible itch to drape the term in scare quotes whenever it crops up. Wittgenstein also points out in the same work that physiology plays a part in our identification of colour. We are constrained in the business of producing a world by natural laws, our physical constitution, existing social practices, our common human nature, the force of custom, convention and tradition and so on.[11] So forms of life are not entirely contingent. They also include features which are common to humanity as such. Every form of life has to make some sense of death, sickness, violence, sexuality and so on.

Grammars, then, must accommodate the sort of creatures we are, as well as the general course of the world, but in Wittgenstein's view they are not grounded in these things. They cannot be justified, any more than playing lacrosse can be justified. The same is true for Wittgenstein of forms of life as a whole, which in the end rest on nothing but themselves. It is only a crippling bout of metaphysical queasiness or ontological anxiety which compels us to slide some stout foundation beneath them, only to find ourselves saddled with the problem of what that foundation is resting on in turn.

Does this then mean that forms of life are sickeningly precarious, afloat in some luminous void? To think so would simply be the flipside of the metaphysician's misgivings. To fear that anything can waft off into the ether at any moment if everything is not permanently nailed down is simply to fall victim to a misleading metaphor. There are those who maintain that without cast-iron necessities and unimpeachable grounds there is nothing but anarchy. If rules are not rigid then they must be unworkably vague. The only alternative to total order is utter chaos. Let a cyclist without a rear light off a fine once and (key phrase) *before you know where you are* the streets of our cities will be thronged with wild-eyed psychopathic killers roaming in search of victims. The anarchist and the authoritarian are terrible twins. The laid-back libertarian is the prodigal son of the paranoid father. It is just that the former rejoices in disorder while the latter abhors it. Otherwise they share the same logic.

Because our concepts are embedded in what Wittgenstein calls "the rough ground" of our everyday life,[12] they are permeated with that roughness themselves. Do we need to measure our distance from the sun down to the nearest foot? Doesn't it make perfect sense to say 'Stand roughly there'? Is a fuzzy image of someone not an image of them at all? It is true that there are times when it is precision, not indeterminacy, that we require. We count 'with merciless exactitude', Wittgenstein points out in his *Remarks on the Foundations of Mathematics*,[13] but this is because the business of counting is so vital to our practical existence. It is what we do which invests some of our language games with a certain stringent necessity, which in Wittgenstein's Nietzschean view we can then come to mistake as a feature of the world itself. Viewed from the outside, games appear arbitrary enough, and it is not hard to feel that we could substitute one for another. Seen from the inside, however, their rules exert a coercive force, which is not to say an unbending one. It is because rules and conventions are embedded in a practical form of life that they have the force they do. If they were purely linguistic they would exercise far less authority over us. To say that one acts conventionally is to say that what bears in on one's behaviour is the activity of others. Language and convention are signs of our solidarity with one another.

* * *

Forms of life, Wittgenstein insists, are simply 'given'. When asked why one does things in a certain way, one can only respond, 'This is simply what I do.' Answers, he maintains, must come to an end somewhere. It is no wonder that he has gained a reputation for conservatism. Yet though he is indeed in some ways a conservative thinker, it is not on this account. To acknowledge the givenness of a form of life is not necessarily to endorse its ethical or political values. 'This is just what we do' is a reasonable enough response when asked why one measures distances in miles rather than kilometres, but not when asked why one administers lethal injections to citizens who are no longer able to work. Forms of life are more anthropological notions than political ones. What is 'given' are practices such as rubbing noses, burying the dead, measuring the distance between human settlements, imagining the future as lying ahead of you or marking in one's language a distinction between various forms of laughter (chortling, braying, simpering, tittering and so on), but not a distinction between an adolescent and pre-adolescent nephew, as some tribal society might feel it appropriate to do.

None of these life-forms is immune to change; but here and now they constitute the context within which our discourse makes sense, and are thus in some provisional sense foundational. A foundation is not necessarily less of a foundation because it might not exist tomorrow or somewhere else in the world. As Wittgenstein remarks in his homespun style, don't claim that there isn't a last house in the road on the grounds that one could always build another.[14]

Indeed one could; but right now *this* is the last one. The subjunctive should not be allowed to trump the indicative. A form of life is a foundation of sorts, though one that the metaphysician might be slow to recognise as such. For one thing, metaphysical foundations are less mutable and open-ended than human cultures, and for another thing they tend to be singular (God, *Geist*, a priori rational principles, phenomenological essences and so on), whereas forms of life are incorrigibly plural.

Morally and politically speaking, Wittgenstein was certainly no apologist for the form of life known as twentieth-century Western civilisation. There is plenty of reason to believe that he was deeply unhappy with the culture of middle-class modernity in which, as a formidably cultivated upper-middle-class Viennese, he found himself stranded. 'An age without culture' is how he once described it.[15] He may not have been a Marxist himself, but some of his best friends were.[16] They included Nikolai Bakhtin, former White Guard, Parisian left-bank bohemian and French Foreign Legionnaire, elder brother of the more celebrated Mikhail and a member of the British Communist Party; the ancient historian George Thomson, later a convert to Maoism and an Irish-language campaigner; the Communist Party economist Maurice Dobb; the Germanist Roy Pascal; and the Italian economist Piero Sraffa, comrade of the imprisoned Antonio Gramsci. Wittgenstein was considered a communist in some Cambridge circles, and confided to a friend that he was indeed one at heart. His lover, Francis Skinner, volunteered to fight with the International Brigade in the Spanish Civil War, but was turned down on medical grounds. Another friend, Frank Ramsay, was rebuked by Wittgenstein as a 'bourgeois' philosopher who shirked a radical break with existing modes of thought.

In 1935, during the ice age of Stalinism, Wittgenstein travelled to the Soviet Union and with typical eccentricity requested permission to become a manual worker there. The authorities were apparently less than enthused by this bizarre proposal. That Wittgenstein was a Stalinist of sorts is not the most well-aired of topics among his admirers, yet it seems to have been the case. His biographer, Ray Monk, is affronted by the suggestion and curtly dismisses it as 'nonsense', while at the same time providing plenty of evidence of his subject's admiration for Stalin's regime.[17] Wittgenstein was unimpressed by talk of labour camps and Soviet tyranny, insisting that those who denounced Stalin had no idea of the problems and dangers he confronted. He continued to look favourably on the Soviet Union even after the show trials and the Nazi–Soviet pact, and claimed that what would most erode his sympathy for the regime would be the growth of class distinctions.[18] He was a member of a university which was later to produce a celebrated clutch of double agents, and though he was clearly no spy himself, he was, like Burgess, Blunt, Maclean, Philby and others, an upper-class dissident.[19] He may have been familiar with some of Marx's work, certainly read the left-wing journal *The New Statesman*, disliked Winston Churchill and intended to vote Labour in the 1945 General Election. He was also troubled by mass unemployment and the threat of fascism. Monk is in no doubt that his sympathies lay with the unemployed, the working class and the political left. 'I was looking at a picture of the British Cabinet,' Wittgenstein acidly remarked, 'and I thought to myself, "a lot of wealthy old men".'[20] It is tempting to detect an Oedipal touch in this disdain, given that Wittgenstein's monstrously authoritarian father was the wealthiest manufacturer in the Austro-Hungarian empire.

If Wittgenstein was attracted to the Soviet Union, it may well have been for largely conservative reasons: his respect for order, discipline and authority; his Tolstoyan idealising of manual labour (at which he himself was remarkably adept); his high-modernist affection for austerity (which he called 'going barefoot', but which in the Russia of the day might more candidly be called destitution); not to speak of his sympathy for a nation that had produced his beloved Dostoevsky along with a precious spiritual heritage. As for idealising manual labour, Wittgenstein regularly exhorted his colleagues and students to give up philosophy and do something useful for a change. When a gifted young disciple took him at his word and spent the rest of his life toiling away in a canning factory, Wittgenstein was said to be overjoyed. He did, to do him justice, try to heed his own advice, fleeing from Cambridge from time to time to some more menial way of life only to be hunted down and taken back into intellectual captivity.

Even so, Marxism was an important if oblique influence on Wittgenstein's later thought. It was Piero Sraffa's critique of bourgeois economics, one which sought to restore its reified categories to their historical contexts, which helped to inspire what one might call the anthropological turn in his colleague's philosophical thought, and which provided the *Investigations* with what Wittgenstein, in the Preface to that work, called its 'most consequential ideas'. It was also Sraffa who made the Neapolitan gesture, fingers swept out from under chin, which played a part in transforming Wittgenstein's conception of language while the two men were travelling together on a train.[21] When it comes to the expressive body, it is hard to outmatch the Italians. If Sraffa supplied the practice, Wittgenstein's friend George Thomson may have provided part of the theory, writing in his study of ancient philosophy of what he takes to be the originally gestural nature of language.[22] Thomson's book deals among other things with the poetic; and poetry is one of the seams between mind and body, as a place where meaning is bound up with such somatic aspects of language as tone, pitch, pace, texture, volume and rhythm. Language is in this sense doubly material: both a sensory medium in itself, and one expressive of the stuff of the body.

Thomson once remarked that Wittgenstein was a Marxist in practice but not in theory. It is hard to see how this could be true of a man who reprimanded strikers for lacking self-discipline and castigated peace campaigners as 'scum'.[23] He also coupled fascism and socialism as among those aspects of modernity which he found 'false and alien'.[24] Wittgenstein may have felt for the plight of the unemployed, but he also ascribed a high value to custom, loyalty, order, reverence, authority and tradition, and condemned revolution as immoral. Nietzsche, for whom the fineness of a soul can be measured by its instinct for reverence, shared much of this outlook, though he would doubtless have regarded Wittgenstein's faith in custom, convention and everyday wisdom as a capitulation to a contemptible 'herd' morality. As a man, Wittgenstein could be haughty, high-handed and tiresomely exacting, with more than a touch of aristocratic hauteur. The generous pluralism of his later thought cuts against the grain of his imperious temperament. Its sociability clashes with his monkish asceticism. He considered the English proverb 'It takes all kinds to make a world' to be a most beautiful and kindly saying, but appears to have found quite a few such kinds profoundly uncongenial.

If Wittgenstein's later thought is quite un-Nietzschean, there was nonetheless a dash of the *Übermensch* about his austere, commanding, nonconformist personality. Like Nietzsche's animal of the future, he was a free, fiercely independent spirit who sought solitude in Nature. Unenthused by the idea of individual freedom, he came under the sway of Oswald Spengler, perhaps the most influential conservative thinker of early twentieth-century Europe.[25] Indeed, much of his social and political thought would seem to stem from the German lineage of so-called *Kulturkritik*, with its hostility to science, progress, liberalism, equality, commercialism, technology, democracy and possessive individualism, its aversion to abstract concepts and utopian visions, all of which prejudices Wittgenstein shared.[26] Generally speaking, gentlemen do not need to justify their existence by anything as low-bred as a theory.

Kulturkritikers, a company which includes Friedrich Nietzsche, speak up for the spontaneous, intuitive wisdom of the aristocrat, in contrast to the desiccated rationalism of the middle classes. Knowledge is more know-how than know-why. For these middle-European traditionalists, everyday life is innocent of the angst, homelessness and spiritual torment which plagues high modernism. Few habits of mind are more foreign to modernism than Wittgenstein's tranquil trust in the ordinary. He is as remote from the turbulence of that movement as the serene, supremely self-assured Goethe is from the psychic turmoil of his Romantic compatriots. Both thinkers are resolutely anti-tragic. Indeed, Wittgenstein writes in *Culture and Value* of the tragic spirit as one alien to him. Moving at ease within the taken-for-granted sphere of one's everyday surroundings, one reaches for one's philosophy only when, by some ruse of language or metaphysical will-o'-the-wisp, there is a danger of losing touch with this perennial source of good sense.

Reason or knowledge may thus be modelled in part on the body, a mode of cognition which is taken to be more primitive and dependable than the mind. I can know where my elbow is at any given moment without needing to use a compass. We have tacit knowledge of the life-world in much the same way that we are intimate with our own flesh. Neither can be totalised or fully objectified, whatever the rationalists may hubristically imagine. As Merleau-Ponty observes, our body 'provides us with a way of access to the word and the object . . . which has to be recognised as original and perhaps primary'.[27] There is a type of somatic understanding which is not reducible to so-called mental representations. There are many cases in which my relation to my body is not a cognitive affair. We do not have knowledge of our own experience, so Wittgenstein insists. Do I know that I am in pain, he enquires? No. So do I not know it? No, once again. The word 'know' simply has no application here. It is like a free-wheeling cog in the machine of language which fails to mesh with anything around it. The verb 'to know' has force only when it is possible not to know, which is not true in this case. I can speak of knowing that you are in pain, since I may be in a position not to know it, but I cannot know that I am.[28]

What is the secret of the seeming contradictions in Wittgenstein's politics? How can one be suspended in this way between Marx and Nietzsche? There seems little doubt that this fastidious traditionalist did indeed hold a range of left-wing views, despite the words of a woman friend who was fearless enough to tell him to his face that Marxism was nothing like as discredited as his own 'antiquated political opinions'.[29] Perhaps some of these leftist convictions faded in later years. But it may also be that his sympathy for Marxism sprang in part from what Raymond Williams has called 'negative identification'.[30] As a conservative, culturally pessimistic critic of middle-class modernity, Wittgenstein felt able to link arms in some respects with his communist colleagues while repudiating their convictions in others. It is a case of adopting one's enemy's enemies as one's friends; or, if one prefers, of the landowner's secret rapport with the poacher, as against the petty-bourgeois gamekeeper. The traditionalist, after all, has a fair amount in common with the socialist. Both camps think in corporate terms, as the liberal individualist or free-marketeer does not. Both regard social life as practical and institutional to its core. In this sense, there is a materialism of the right as well as of the left. Neither party is much enthused by the capitalist marketplace or parliamentary democracy. Both view human relations as the matrix of personal identity, not as an infringement of it. Both seek to chastise a rationality that has grown too big for its boots, returning it to its proper place within social existence as a whole. If Marxists like Bakhtin and Sraffa reject the present in the name of the future, Wittgenstein may have spurned it in the name of the past.

Is the later Wittgenstein's thought, then, an expression of his conservatism? It is true that as a philosopher he thinks in terms of customs and conventions, of ingrained dispositions and well-entrenched forms of behaviour. And this inclination is doubtless shaped to some extent by his broader social views. Yet there is nothing necessarily conservative about such a case. A socialist society would also work by habitual beliefs and well-embedded forms of practice, at least if it had been in business long enough. It is not as though everything would be perpetually up for debate. Self-governing cooperatives work just as much by custom and convention as Buckingham Palace garden parties. Left-wing societies value their historical legacies as much as right-wing ones. Indeed, it was Leon Trotsky who remarked that revolutionaries like himself had always lived in tradition. If a reverence for authority is a sort of second nature for conservatives, a scepticism of it may feel much the same for their radical opponents.

All the same, Wittgenstein's conservatism does indeed place limits on his thought. It is not true, as he claims, that to resolve our problems we simply need to rearrange what we already know. Indeed, it is blatantly, laughably false. Nor is it true, as he suggests, that someone seeking an answer to such questions is like a man imprisoned in a room without realising that the door is unlocked but he needs to pull rather than push.[31] There is a glibness about such talk which grates. It smacks too much of the donnish complacency which Wittgenstein despised, yet some of whose more unsavoury habits of mind he came to adopt. In any case, what of the conflicts and contradictions inherent in a form of life? Are there not times when consensus is thrown into disarray? Cannot customs and conventions be subject to ferocious dispute? 'It is characteristic of our language,' writes Fergus Kerr in a paraphrase of Wittgenstein's case, 'that it springs up on the foundation of stable forms of life, regular ways of acting.'[32] But forms of life are not always stable or ways of acting regular, not least in periods of political turmoil. Wittgenstein himself lived through just such an era – one in which a social and political crisis of titanic proportions made its presence felt among other places in that confounding of stability and regularity we know as modernism. Perhaps his affection for custom and tradition was in part compensation for this historical upheaval, a twinge of nostalgia for a less contentious age.

It is a striking feature of modernity that we find ourselves unable to agree even on fundamentals. Almost everyone takes the view that attempting to asphyxiate the various small children we encounter on the street is not a course of action to be commended, but we cannot agree on why we agree on this, and perhaps never will. Liberal pluralism may involve striking a pact with those whose views we utterly repudiate. One of the prices we pay for liberty is having to put up with a lot of ideological garbage. In this sense, at least, there is certainly no concurrence within forms of life. One might retort that this is to mistake the essentially anthropological notion of a form of life for moral or political unanimity. Even so, Wittgenstein's social conservatism can lead him to underplay discord and antagonism, projecting the anthropological on to the political. The idea of *structural* conflict would seem quite foreign to him. It is hard to shake off the suspicion that when he thinks of a form of life, it is a tribe or rural village that he has in mind rather than an advanced industrial society. It is true that forms of life cut deeper than moral or political strife, in the sense that (for example) both parties to the English Civil War multiplied and subtracted in the same manner, distinguished between animate and inanimate objects, and thought of the past as lying behind them. In fact, unless the two sides shared a number of basic categories in common, they could not be said to have clashed, since conflict presupposes a degree of common ground. Yet the political and anthropological may not always be so easily distinguished. In any case, there may also be contentions at the 'anthropological' level. Perhaps different life-forms can overlap in some ways but not in others. There may be a bunch of people down the road who share our own ways of doing things enough to pay income tax and use public transport, but who see their bodies as spun out of some exquisitely fine, glass-like substance and perceive evil spirits squatting on our shoulders.

* * *

There is no concept of ideology in Wittgenstein's work. It is true that he is much concerned with what one might call false consciousness – with the various metaphysical illusions bred by our language and form of life. But he has no conception of what Jürgen Habermas has called 'systematically distorted communication',[33] let alone the relation of this to political power. In his view, our language is in order just as it is, even if it generates from time to time those pseudo-problems which it is the task of philosophy to dispel. These conundrums are not primarily to be seen as in the service of power, which is how Marx views ideology. They have no particular function in social life, though they may well have a foundation in it, as we shall see in a moment.

All the same, there is a clear parallel between Wittgenstein's style of philosophising and the Marxist critique of ideology. It is not as though the former deals with language while the latter addresses real life. We have seen already that for Wittgenstein there can be no clear distinction between the two. 'The problems of philosophy,' one Wittgenstein scholar remarks, 'have their roots in a distortion or malfunction of the language-games which in its turn signalizes that something is wrong with the ways in which men live.'[34] Wittgenstein's celebrated insistence that our language is in order just as it is can be read as smugly self-satisfied; but it may also constitute a materialist rebuke to the callow intellectualism which hopes to repair human ills by rearranging our speech or refurbishing our ideas. Language is in order in so far as it registers what is amiss with our form of life as well as what is affirmative about it. In any other sense of the term, it is far from being in good shape.

Treating a philosophical problem, Wittgenstein remarks in the *Investigations*, is like treating an illness. 'It is possible,' he writes in his *Remarks on the Foundations of Mathematics*, 'for the sickness of philosophical problems to get cured only through a changed mode of thought and of life, not through a medicine invented by an individual.'[35] Marx might have said just the same of ideology. For both thinkers, such conceptual problems are symptomatic, rather as the neurotic symptom for Freud marks the site of some pathological disturbance in everyday life – one which, like ideology, it both reveals and conceals. We have seen already that Nietzsche regards morality itself as a kind of sign-language or symptomatology. Marx, Nietzsche, Freud and Wittgenstein are not in the business of treating symptoms. Instead, they seek to tackle the root cause of the disorder, which means approaching its various expressions in diagnostic spirit. Only through a change of behaviour might some of our conceptual snarl-ups be consigned to the ashcan of history. 'I am by no means sure,' Wittgenstein comments, 'that I should prefer a continuation of my work by others to a change in the way people live which would make all these questions superfluous.'[36]

The change he has in mind is not primarily a political one. Whereas Marx sees practices as systemic, so that a deep enough alteration in what we do must involve structural transformation, Wittgenstein does not view the world in this light. Yet the society which breeds some of the illusions Wittgenstein seeks to demystify is one that Marx would assuredly have recognised. It is bourgeois individualism, among various other sources of delusion, that the patrician Wittgenstein has in his sights, though he would most certainly not have used the term himself, or imagined that socialism was any satisfying solution to it. What he is out to contest among other things is the image of the self-transparent subject in undisputed possession of its private experience, trusting that the truth of things lies securely anchored in this privileged realm, cut off by the walls of its body from other selves and from the world, and thus given to a certain scepticism as to their ontological solidity. For this immaterial, self-constituting ego, language, social relations and its own flesh and blood are secondary phenomena, bits of the public world only contingently related to it. Its defiant cry is 'You can't have my experiences!' But as one commentator points out, it is neither true nor false that you cannot have my experiences, since the phrase 'to have someone else's experience' is meaningless.[37] In the sense of the word 'have' at stake here, I do not have my own experiences either. Or not have them, for that matter.

In Wittgenstein's view, metaphysical forms of thought are falsely homogenising, conflating phenomena that need to be distinguished. He considered that most of our errors arose from this habit, and that it was differences we needed to discern. Some Marxist thinkers, not least Georg Lukács and the luminaries of the Frankfurt School, have sought in similar spirit to reveal what they see as the formalising, homogenising, universalising features of bourgeois thought, and have traced its sources to the structures of capitalism. Wittgenstein's colleague George Thomson does just this in *The First Philosophers*, which tracks the roots of philosophy to commodity exchange. There is a distinctively 'vulgar' Marxist quality to this, of which Wittgenstein himself is quite innocent. All the same, he seems to have perceived a relation between certain typical philosophical blunders and the modern civilisation he found so distasteful.

Persuading people to change how they live is no simple matter. Men and women, Wittgenstein believes, are sunk deep in mental confusion, and to free them from this condition means 'tearing them away from the enormous number of connecting links that hold them fast. A sort of rearrangement of the whole of their language is needed.' So radical is this emancipation that it 'will succeed only with those in whose life there is already an instinctive rebellion against the language in question and not with those whose whole instinct is for life in the very herd that created that language as its proper expression'.[38] The thinker who has been accused of consecrating the hackneyed wisdom of everyday life rounds upon it here with a Nietzschean snarl ('herd'). The political metaphor of rebellion, the violence of 'tearing away', the sense of a profound

143

antagonism between the conformist 'herd' and those capable of enlightenment: this is scarcely the language of a champion of common sense. Indeed, Wittgenstein explicitly disowns any such philosophical populism. You must not try to avoid a philosophical problem by appealing to common sense, he remarks, but allow yourself to be dragged fully into the difficulty so that you might eventually fight your way out of it.[39] In this sense, he is far from being an 'ordinary language' philosopher. He would not, one imagines, have been much impressed by Gilbert Ryle's claim to have argued an Oxford undergraduate out of committing suicide by pointing out to him that the grammar of 'nothing matters' differs from that of 'nothing chatters'. On the contrary, he sees so-called ordinary language as full of mirages: 'In our language there is an entire mythology embedded.'[40]

For Marx, the proletariat can be emancipated by nobody but itself, while for Freud it is the patient who must perform most of the hard psychoanalytic labour. For his part, the later Wittgenstein sees the task of the philosopher not as delivering the truth head-on, a strategy which would reduce philosophy to a purely theoretical affair, but as presenting readers with a series of jokes, images, anecdotes, exclamations, ironic queries, wonderings aloud, snatches of dialogue and unanswered questions, so that they may attain the koan-like point at which illumination breaks upon them and they see the world in a new light. It is a set of tactics which Søren Kierkegaard also deploys, under the title of 'indirection'. 'The only correct method of doing philosophy,' Wittgenstein remarks, 'consists in not saying anything and leaving it to another person to make a claim . . . I simply draw the other person's attention to what he is really doing and refrain from making assertions.'[41] It is a wonder that he did not lay his colleagues and students on couches rather than seat them in deckchairs, as was his custom.

For Freud, psychoanalysis is a practice, not in the first place a theoretical discourse; for Wittgenstein, philosophy is a practice and not a theoretical discourse at all. Like psychoanalysis or the Marxist critique of ideology, it is a demythologising activity, a therapy held in store for particularly grievous cases of mystification. We must use it, Wittgenstein insists, against philosophy and 'the philosopher in us'.[42] We are all spontaneous metaphysicians, dupes of the false consciousness built into our language and forms of life. If the philosopher and psychoanalyst are guaranteed never to go out of business, it is not because they teach imperishable truths but because fantasy and delusion are as endemic to humankind as influenza. Like physicians, philosophers render their services superfluous over and over again. How then can the task of philosophy, as Wittgenstein sometimes suggests, be simply to lead words back from their metaphysical to their everyday uses when everyday life is itself shot through with metaphysical illusions?

Despite his dark suspicions of philosophy, Wittgenstein is gracious enough to concede it a limited value. To change the world, he believes, you have to change the way you look at it, and philosophy can be useful in this respect.[43] Yet, though changing the way you look at things is a necessary condition for changing them in reality, it is not in Wittgenstein's view a sufficient one, any more than it is for Marx. This is why he infamously insists that philosophy leaves everything just as it was. Its task is not to furnish our ways of talking with a foundation, since they have one already in our form of life. How absurdly idealist to imagine that it is *philosophers* who can transform our activity! 'That man will be revolutionary who can first revolutionise himself', Wittgenstein comments,[44] and a philosopher can no more do this for you than he can sneeze on your behalf. Like yawning or vomiting, emancipation is something you have to do for yourself. It is certainly something that Wittgenstein tried to do for himself. As one afflicted with that strange form of mania known as the Protestant conscience, for him the need to reconstruct one's life was no hollow piety. As the son of a fabulously rich industrialist, he gave away most of his considerable fortune and in the course of his riches-to-rags career shifted between spells as an aeronautical engineer, an amateur architect, a Cambridge academic, a village schoolmaster, a monastery gardener, a hermit in Norway and a recluse in the west of Ireland. In all of this, he displayed an exemplary moral courage and integrity. His disdain for dons was no donnish affectation.

That your emancipation is up to you is a belief that Wittgenstein shared with Marx. That they differ in other respects is plain enough. Wittgenstein was too moral by half, while Marx was too little so, dismissing morality as so much ideology. The change of life that for Wittgenstein might throw philosophers onto the job market is for the most part a personal and ethical affair, whereas for Marx it is collective and political. Marx believes that thought must penetrate the false appearances of social reality to grasp the hidden mechanisms which generate it, whereas Wittgenstein rejects any such notion of concealed depths, along with the need for explanatory theories. He does not of course deny that there are things that are concealed, but he rejects the notion that there is a pervasive gap between appearances and reality. Discrepancies between the two are local rather than structural. Depth, in the sense of something permanently lurking beneath what we perceive, is part of the problem rather than the solution. It is what we read into reality rather than pluck out of it. Indeed, it is because the truth is so obvious that we fail to notice it, whereas for Marxism the obvious is the very homeland of ideology. For the author of *Capital*, the way social life appears at present is askew to the way it actually is. Semblance is built into its substance. It is not just a matter of our misperceptions. Wittgenstein does not see the world as stratified in this manner, and the claim that there is a structural gap between appearance and reality would doubtless strike him as a metaphysical illusion. On the contrary, it is our failure to perceive what lies beneath our noses that leads us astray. Instead, we project behind it some impalpable domain (soul, will, essence, consciousness, mental process, unimpeachable foundations and so on) which then comes to constitute its secret truth. In this respect, Wittgenstein is strikingly close to Nietzsche. For Nietzsche, there is nothing behind appearances at all, in which case we might as well stop talking about appearances.

It is this hypostasising – this itch to turn human faculties and activities into invisible substances – that Marx, Nietzsche and Wittgenstein all spurn as metaphysical. For the Marxist heritage, it is a hypostasis more commonly known as reification, a condition in which thinghood becomes the measure of reality. For Marx, capital is a relation, not a thing, and the same is true of social class; labour is an open-ended capacity rather than a determinate entity; the state is a means for regulating conflict, not the locus of the spirit of the nation; and history is simply the multifarious actions of men and women, with no sublime purposes of its own. It is idols and fetishes which all three men have in their sights, as certain activities and capabilities are prised loose from everyday life and come to assume a minatory power of their own. Marx was not to know that this fate would befall his own thought not long after his death, as a critique of ideology became a prime example of it.

Philosophy, then, is really a form of iconoclasm. In *Ecce Homo*, Nietzsche declares the overthrow of idols to be a vital part of his task.[45] A hammer, he believes, is among the philosopher's most precious tools. True to this spirit, Wittgenstein remarks that 'All that philosophy can do is destroy idols.'[46] It must free up human thought by dispelling certain reified conceptions that have gained a lethal grip over us. 'Philosophers,' he complains, 'as it were freeze language and make it rigid.'[47] Freud argues a similar case about pathological human behaviour, in which it is one's actions that become rigid and unbending. (Wittgenstein himself seems to have been afflicted with such a neurosis. He was physically rigid and unbending as well as morally so. He felt that his knees were stiff, and that if he knelt to pray he might go soft and dissolve away.[48] There have been less exotic excuses for not going to church.)

There are other connections between the apparently abstruse sphere of metaphysics and everyday life. The belief that there are immutable essences and self-evident foundations; that we can break reality down to certain irreducible components; that the existence of the world can be indubitably demonstrated; that all of our practices need to be rationally justified; that there might be a rule that would regulate all other rules; that I can know my own experience for certain; that there is a pre-established harmony between language and reality; that definitions and distinctions which are not absolutely watertight are not definitions and distinctions at all: all this, as both Nietzsche and Wittgenstein recognise, betokens a deep-seated anxiety and insecurity, along with a countervailing drive to command and control. It is in this sense that we can speak of the politics of the metaphysical. What seems to stand at the most majestic remove from practical existence turns out to be on unsettlingly close terms with it.

The resolution of theoretical contradictions, Marx writes in his *Economic and Philosophical Manuscripts*, is possible only through practical means. 'All mysteries which lead to mysticism,' he declares in his eighth thesis on Feuerbach, 'find their rational solution in human practice and in the comprehension of that practice' – a claim which would not be out of place in the later Wittgenstein. We have already taken leave to query this conviction. There are plenty of philosophical puzzles that cannot be unmasked as practical problems in conceptual disguise, and which refuse to slink obediently away simply because their origins have been traced to a material form of life. In any case, if forms of life are inherently inclined to fostering false consciousness, they would appear to be as much part of the problem as the solution. Marx can imagine a future free of these impostures because in his view ideology has a strictly provisional existence. Since its function is to intervene in the class-struggle at the level of ideas, weighing in on the side of the sovereign powers, it will disappear once that authority is ousted. For Wittgenstein, by contrast, there can be no closure to the reign of metaphysics, a view he shares with Jacques Derrida.[49] Even were we to demythologise our thought by changing the way we live, language would no doubt be standing by to breed in us yet more spiritual sickness. There can, however, be a series of guerrilla raids on this implacable power, a set of skirmishes known as philosophy.

* * *

Wittgenstein speaks in the *Investigations* of what he calls the 'natural history' of human beings, and comments elsewhere that 'I want to regard man here as an animal'.[50] It is a viewpoint we have already encountered in Aquinas, Marx and Nietzsche. He also writes of everyday certainty as 'something that lies beyond being justified or unjustified; as it were, as something animal'.[51] It is not by recourse to theory that we know there is a tarantula under the toast rack. In this sense, Wittgenstein's scepticism of theory is not simply old-style mandarin prejudice, though it is that as well. It is bound up with his materialism. A good deal of our knowledge is carnal knowledge, grounded in our bodily responses. When Wittgenstein writes in the *Investigations* of how we obey rules 'blindly', he is not out to foster a craven subservience to authority but, once again, to anchor thought in the body. To cross the road the moment the little green figure begins to flash is a sign of the fact that our relationship to the world is not primarily a theoretical one. We follow the signal blindly, which is not to say irrationally. Obeying it so unthinkingly is part of the way we have internalised the shared conventions which govern our form of life, converting them into bodily disposition. We do not need to 'interpret' the sign. The idea that we are perpetually engaged in the business of interpretation is the misconception of those who spend too much of their time reading Ezra Pound.

Language, Wittgenstein argues, is tied to certain facts of nature, not least to our bodily behaviour. We have a range of natural, instinctive responses to others (fear, pity, disgust, compassion and so on) which eventually enter into our moral and political language-games but which are in themselves prior to interpretation. And these responses, belonging as they do to the natural history of humanity, are universal in nature. They are part of what it means to be a human body, however much any specific body may be culturally conditioned. It is on this material foundation that the most durable forms of human solidarity can be built. Imagine trying to learn the language of a culture very different from our own. We would observe how its members cook, joke, worship, mend their garments, punish transgressors and so on, and in doing so could find a foothold for understanding their forms of speech in so far as they are bound up with these activities. Yet much of this depends on sharing the same physical constitution as they do – on what Wittgenstein calls the 'natural expressiveness' of the human body. If they respond to having their legs cut off at the knees without anaesthetic by delivering magnificently eloquent lectures on their cosmological beliefs, complete with erudite allusions and entertaining asides, getting to understand them would seem an uphill task. We might do better dating a rabbit. As Fergus Kerr observes, 'it is our bodiliness which founds our being able, in principle, to learn any natural language on earth'.[52]

Wittgenstein's conception of philosophy is unduly modest. It can be more than a therapy for mystified minds. Yet in seeking to undercut its pretensions, he reveals a respect for the mundane world which is unusual among the intelligentsia, including some leftist intellectuals today. There is a necessary tension in socialist thought between affirming everyday experience and distrusting it. If thinkers like Raymond Williams and Jürgen Habermas might be said to lean too far in the former direction, a range of leftist luminaries who emerged in their wake too often denigrate what Wittgenstein calls the common behaviour of humanity, scorning the very notion as incorrigibly ideological. In this mode of thought, consensus, convention, common morality and workaday institutions come off badly in contrast with some more privileged domain (the Real, the Event, desire, the political, the semiotic, the ethical decision, the revolutionary act, the 'impossible', the gratuitous gesture and so on). It is a peculiarly French vice, exemplified in our own time by the otherwise path-breaking work of Alain Badiou. The question of whether, given such a jaundiced view of the commonplace, humanity is worth revolutionising in the first place is then as hard to avoid as it is to answer.

Antonio Gramsci, political comrade of Wittgenstein's friend Piero Sraffa, is in search of a critique of everyday practice which would not simply upbraid it from some metaphysical height, but which would also do more than merely consecrate popular prejudice. Instead, it would seek out what was already critical in a form of life, not least the sense of agency and transformative possibility implicit in its workaday activities, and elaborate it to the point where it might constitute an alternative form of 'common sense'.[53] Something similar might be said of Wittgenstein. In his patrician style, he can indeed be too credulous about established practice. At his finest, however, he combines an artist's sensitivity to the common life with a prophet's insistence that ordinary men and women must be torn from their attachment to self-serving fantasises. It is a rare enough equipoise.

Notes

1 Materialisms

1. For materialist thought in the eighteenth century, see John W. Yolton, *Thinking Matter: Materialism in Eighteenth-Century Britain* (Oxford: Basil Blackwell, 1984).
2. See Raymond Williams, *Keywords: A Vocabulary of Culture and Society* (revised edition, London: Fontana, 1983), p. 199.
3. Friedrich Engels, *The Dialectics of Nature* (New York: International Publishers, 1940), pp. 291–2.
4. Sigmund Freud, 'Project for a Scientific Psychology', in Ernst Kris (ed.), *The Origins of Psychoanalysis* (New York: Basic Books, 1954), p. 379.
5. Sebastiano Timpanaro, *On Materialism* (London: New Left Books, 1975), p. 36.
6. For an example of Marxist orthodoxy on this question, see Antonio Labriola, *Essays on the Materialistic Conception of History* (London: Monthly Review Press, 1966).
7. For an orthodox account, see Henri Lefebvre, *Dialectical Materialism* (London: Jonathan Cape, 1968).
8. The view that dialectical materialism is a form of idealism rests on the charge that it projects the properly mental or linguistic operations of negation, contradiction and so on into material reality itself. For this argument see Lucio Colletti, *Marxism and Hegel* (London: New Left Books, 1973), Part 1.

9. See John Milbank, 'Materialism and Transcendence', in Creston Davis, John Milbank and Slavoj Žižek (eds), *Theology and the Political* (Durham, NC: Duke University Press, 2005), pp. 394–5.

10. Slavoj Žižek, *Absolute Recoil: Towards a New Foundation of Dialectical Materialism* (London: Verso, 2014), p. 13.

11. Introduction to Diana Cook and Samantha Frost (eds), *New Materialisms: Ontology, Agency, and Politics* (Durham, NC: Duke University Press, 2010), p. 9.

12. Jane Bennett, 'A Vitalist Stopover on the Way to a New Materialism', ibid., p. 47. See also her full-length study *Vibrant Matter* (Durham, NC: Duke University Press, 2010) for an admirably complete statement of the case.

13. Pheng Cheah, 'Non-Dialectical Materialism', in Cook and Frost (eds), *New Materialisms*, p. 79.

14. Rey Chow, 'The Elusive Material: What the Dog Doesn't Understand', ibid., p. 226.

15. Eric L. Santner, *The Weight of All Flesh: On the Subject-Matter of Political Economy* (Oxford: Oxford University Press, 2016), p. 261.

16. Karl Marx, *Early Writings* (London: Penguin, 1992), p. 328.

17. For an excellent guide to Deleuze's work, see Peter Hallward, *Deleuze and the Philosophy of Creation* (London: Verso, 2006).

18. See in particular Raymond Williams, *Culture* (London: Fontana, 1981) and *Culture and Materialism* (London: Verso, 2005). For a useful account, see Andrew Milner, *Cultural Materialism* (Melbourne: Melbourne University Press, 1993).

19. Ludwig Wittgenstein, *The Blue and Brown Books* (Oxford: Basil Blackwell, 1958), p. 3.

20. See Anthony Kenny, *Wittgenstein* (Harmondsworth: Penguin, 1973), Ch. 8.

21. Karl Marx, *Early Writings*, p. 356.

22. Karl Marx and Friedrich Engels, *The German Ideology* (London: Lawrence and Wishart, 1974), pp. 50–1.

23. Ibid.

24. See Samantha Frost, 'Fear and the Illusion of Autonomy', in *New Materialisms*, pp. 158–76.

25. Joeri Schrijvers, *An Introduction to Jean-Yves Lacoste* (Farnham: Ashgate, 1988), p. 49.

26. Timpanaro, *On Materialism*, p. 34.

27. Marx, *Early Writings*, p. 389.

28. See Jean-Luc Nancy, *The Sense of the World* (Minneapolis: University of Minnesota Press, 1997), p. 34.

29. See Simon Critchley, *Infinitely Demanding: Ethics of Commitment, Politics of Resistance* (London: Verso, 2012), p. 86.

30. Alfred Schmidt, *The Concept of Nature in Marx* (London: New Left Books, 1971), p. 96.

31. For an account of the extraordinary psychopathology of the Wittgenstein family, see Alexander Waugh, *The House of Wittgenstein: A Family at War* (London: Bloomsbury, 2008).

32. Ludwig Wittgenstein, *Culture and Value* (Oxford: Blackwell, 1980), p. 4e.

33. For an absorbing study of Freud and Wittgenstein's Vienna, see Allan Janik and Stephen Toulmin, *Wittgenstein's Vienna* (New York: Simon & Schuster, 1973), a work which refers at one point to 'Leonard Woolf's wife, Virginia'. For Wittgenstein and Freud, see Brian McGuinness, 'Freud and Wittgenstein', in Brian McGuinness (ed.), *Wittgenstein and his Times* (Bristol: Theommes Press, 1998), pp. 108–20.

34. See in particular his *After Finitude: An Essay on the Necessity of Contingency* (London: Continuum, 2009). Useful studies of Meillassoux's thought are Levi Bryant, Nick Srnicek and Graham Harman (eds), *The Speculative Turn: Continental Materialism and Realism* (Melbourne: re.press, 2011), Christopher Watkin, *Difficult Atheism* (Edinburgh: Edinburgh University Press, 2011) and Graham Harman, *Quentin Meillassoux: Philosophy in the Making* (Edinburgh: Edinburgh University Press, 2011).

35. Spinoza, *Ethics* (London: Everyman, 1993), p. 25.

36. In Harman, *Quentin Meillassoux: Philosophy in the Making*, pp. 90–122.

37. Friedrich Engels, *Ludwig Feuerbach and the End of Classical German Philosophy* (London: Union Books, 2009), p. 30.

2 Do Badgers Have Souls?

1. Ludwig Wittgenstein, *Philosophical Investigations* (Oxford: Basil Blackwell, 1967), p. 178. In some of what follows I draw on my article 'The Body as Language', *Canadian Review of Comparative Literature*, 41, 1 (March, 2014), pp. 11–16.

2. Maurice Merleau-Ponty, *Phenomenology of Perception* (London: Routledge, 1962), p. 94.

3. See Karl Marx and Friedrich Engels, *Collected Works*, vol. 5 (London: Lawrence & Wishart, 1976), p. 44.

4. Denys Turner, *Thomas Aquinas: A Portrait* (New Haven, CT: Yale University Press, 2013), p. 62.

5. See Ludwig Wittgenstein, *Zettel*, ed. G.E.M. Anscombe and G.H. von Wright (Oxford: Basil Blackwell, 1967), p. 220.

6. Marx, *Early Writings*, p. 355.

7. Wittgenstein, *Philosophical Investigations*, p. 178.

8. Nancy, *The Sense of the World*, p. 131.

9. Engels and Marx, *The German Ideology*, pp. 55–6.

10. See Nicholas M. Heaney, *Thomas Aquinas: Theologian of the Christian Life* (Aldershot: Ashgate, 2003), pp. 140–1. For Aquinas's views on soul and body, see in particular Ralph McInerny (ed.), *Aquinas Against the Averroists* (Lafayette, IN: Purdue University Press, 1993) and Thomas Aquinas, *Light of Faith: The Compendium of Theology* (Manchester, NH: Sophia Institute, 1993). For some rather less world-shaking comments on the theology of the body, see Terry Eagleton, *The Body as Language: Outline of a 'New Left' Theology* (London: Sheed & Ward, 1970).

11. Alasdair MacIntyre, *Dependent Rational Animals* (London: Duckworth, 1999), p. 49.

12. Marx, *Early Writings*, p. 355.

13. Ibid., p. 328.

14. Merleau-Ponty, *Phenomenology of Perception*, p. 102.

15. See Wittgenstein, *Zettel*, para. 504.

16. Friedrich Nietzsche, *The Twilight of the Idols* and *The Anti-Christ* (Harmondsworth: Penguin, 1968), p. 151.

17. Turner, *Thomas Aquinas*, p. 52.

18. Ibid., p. 51.

19. Ibid., p. 90.

20. Ibid., p. 97.

21. Ibid., p. 89.

22. Giorgio Agamben, *The Open: Man and Animal* (Stanford, CA: Stanford University Press, 2004).

23. Wittgenstein, *Philosophical Investigations*, p. 223.

24. See MacIntyre, *Dependent Rational Animals*, p. 59.

25. Martin Heidegger, *The Fundamental Concepts of Metaphysics* (Bloomington, IN: University of Indiana Press, 1955), p. 210.

26. See John Macmurray, *Reason and Emotion* (London: Faber & Faber, 1962), p. 7.

27. See Terry Eagleton, *The Ideology of the Aesthetic* (Oxford: Wiley-Blackwell, 1990), Ch. 1.

28. See Alasdair MacIntyre, *After Virtue* (Notre Dame, IN: University of Notre Dame Press, 1981).

3 Emancipating the Senses

1. 'Theses on Feuerbach', in Marx and Engels, *The German Ideology*, p. 121.

2. Marx, *Early Writings*, p. 352.

3. I have discussed these issues further in my 'Bodies, Artworks, and Use Values', *New Literary History*, 44, 4 (Autumn, 2013), pp. 561–73.

4. Engels and Marx, *The German Ideology*, p. 62.

5. Marx, *Early Writings*, p. 354 (translation slightly amended).

6. Ibid., p. 352.

7. Jürgen Habermas, *Knowledge and Human Interests* (Cambridge: Polity, 1987), pp. 35–6. For an excellent critique of Marx's work in this respect, one which rebukes his early denigration of both science and objectivity, see Andrew Feenberg, *The Philosophy of Praxis: Marx, Lukács and the Frankfurt School* (London: Verso, 2014), especially Ch. 3.

8. Habermas, *Knowledge and Human Interests*, p. 41.

9. Engels and Marx, *The German Ideology*, p. 50.

10. Ibid., p. 50. For a useful discussion of this topic, see John Bellamy Foster, *Marx's Ecology: Materialism and Nature* (New York: Monthly Review Press, 2000).

11. Engels and Marx, *The German Ideology*, p. 63.

12. Timpanaro, *On Materialism*, p. 50.

13. John Macmurray, *The Self as Agent* (London: Faber & Faber, 1969), p. 101. Macmurray's thought runs counter to Anglo-Saxon philosophical orthodoxy in its historicism and communitarianism. The same is true of Alasdair MacIntyre, a speaker of both Scots and Irish Gaelic, as well as of some other Irish and Scottish thinkers. It is less easy to ignore questions of history and community on the colonial margins.

14. Marx, *Early Writings*, p. 328.

15. Engels and Marx, *The German Ideology*, p. 42.

16. See Norman Geras, *Marx and Human Nature: Refutation of a Legend* (London: Verso, 1983), a work which argues that Marx did indeed have a concept of human nature and that he was quite right to do so.

17. Kate Soper, 'Marxism, Materialism and Biology', in John Mepham and David-Hillel Ruben (eds), *Issues in Marxist Philosophy*, vol. 2 (Brighton: Harvester, 1979), p. 95.

18. Raymond Williams, 'Problems of Materialism', *New Left Review*, 109 (May–June,1978), p. 14.

19. Engels and Marx, *The German Ideology*, p. 49 (translation slightly amended).

20. Marx, *Early Writings*, p. 352.

21. Ibid., p. 238.

22. Ibid., pp. 360 and 285.

23. Ibid., p. 361.

24. Ibid.

25. Elaine Scarry, *The Body in Pain* (Oxford: Oxford University Press, 1987), p. 244.

26. Marx, *Early Writings*, p. 329.

27. Ibid., p. 351.

28. Ibid., p. 365.

29. Engels and Marx, *The German Ideology*, p. 47 (translation amended).

30. Theodor Adorno, *Negative Dialectics* (London: Routledge & Kegan Paul, 1973), p. 408.

31. Macmurray, *The Self as Agent*, p. 25.

32. Nietzsche, *Twilight of the Idols* and *The Anti-Christ*, p. 35.

33. Walter Benjamin, *Illuminations*, ed. Hannah Arendt (London: Fontana, 1973), pp. 256–7.

34. Engels and Marx, *The German Ideology*, pp. 51–2.

35. Quoted by Alfred Schmidt, *The Concept of Nature in Marx* (London: New Left Books, 1971), pp. 31–2.

36. Etienne Balibar, *The Philosophy of Marx* (London: Verso, 1995), p. 2.

37. *Basic Writings of Nietzsche*, ed. Walter Kaufmann (New York: Random House, 1968), p. 737.

38. Quoted in Schmidt, *The Concept of Nature in Marx*, p. 24.

39. G.E. Moore, 'Wittgenstein's Lectures in 1930–33', in *Philosophical Papers* (London: Allen & Unwin, 1959), p. 322.

40. Richard Rorty, *Consequences of Pragmatism* (Brighton: Harvester Press, 1982), p. 93.

41. For a suggestive comparison of the two thinkers, see D. Rubinstein, *Marx and Wittgenstein: Social Praxis and Social Explanation* (London: Routledge & Kegan Paul, 1981).

42. Engels and Marx, *The German Ideology*, p. 118.

4 High Spirits

1. Friedrich Nietzsche, *Beyond Good and Evil*, in *Basic Writings of Nietzsche*, p. 393. The finest introduction to Nietzsche's thought is Richard Schacht's detailed, judicious, comprehensive *Nietzsche* (London: Routledge and Kegan Paul, 1983).

2. Nietzsche, *Beyond Good and Evil*, in *Basic Writings of Nietzsche*, p. 307.

3. Ibid., p. 534.

4. Theodor Adorno, *Prisms* (London: Neville Spearman, 1967), p. 260.

5. For a valuable account of Nietzsche and art, see Alexander Nehamas, *Nietzsche: Life as Literature* (Cambridge, MA: Harvard University Press, 1985).

6. Nietzsche, *The Twilight of the Idols* and *The Anti-Christ*, p. 116.

7. Ludwig Wittgenstein, *Remarks on the Philosophy of Psychology* (Oxford: Basil Blackwell, 1980), vol. 2, p. 690.

8. Friedrich Nietzsche, *Thus Spake Zarathustra* (London: Penguin, 2003), pp. 61–2.

9. Nietzsche, *The Twilight of the Idols* and *The Anti-Christ*, p. 124.

10. Friedrich Nietzsche, *The Gay Science* (New York: Vintage, 1974), p. 18.

11. Ibid., p. 267.

12. Friedrich Nietzsche, *The Will to Power* (New York: Vintage, 1967), p. 284.

13. Friedrich Nietzsche, *Daybreak: Thoughts on the Prejudices of Morality* (Cambridge: Cambridge University Press, 1997), p. 76.

14. Nietzsche, *On the Genealogy of Morals*, in *Basic Writings of Nietzsche*, p. 544.

15. Nietzsche, *Beyond Good and Evil*, in *Basic Writings of Nietzsche*, p. 323.

16. Nietzsche, *Ecce Homo*, in *Basic Writings of Nietzsche*, p. 689.

17. Nietzsche, *Beyond Good and Evil*, in *Basic Writings of Nietzsche*, p. 202.

18. Ibid., p. 237.

19. Nietzsche, *On the Genealogy of Morals*, in *Basic Writings of Nietzsche*, p. 531.

20. Ibid., p. 529.

21. Ibid., p. 498.

22. Sigmund Freud, *The Future of an Illusion*, in *Sigmund Freud*, vol. 12, *Civilization, Society and Religion* (Harmondsworth: Penguin, 1985), p. 192.

23. Nietzsche, *Beyond Good and Evil*, in *Basic Writings of Nietzsche*, p. 392.
24. Quoted in Andrew Bowie, *Aesthetics and Subjectivity: From Kant to Nietzsche* (Manchester: Manchester University Press, 1990), p. 224 (translation slightly amended).
25. I have discussed this subject in more detail in *Culture and the Death of God* (New Haven, CT: Yale University Press, 2014), Ch. 5.
26. See, for this tradition of social thought, Raymond Williams, *Culture and Society 1780–1950* (Nottingham: Spokesman Books, 2013).

5 The Rough Ground

1. Ludwig Wittgenstein, *On Certainty* (Oxford: Basil Blackwell, 1969), p. 23.
2. A.C. Grayling, *Wittgenstein* (Oxford: Oxford University Press, 1988), p. 84.
3. MacIntyre, *Dependent Rational Animals*, p. 30.
4. Nietzsche, *Beyond Good and Evil*, in *Basic Writings of Nietzsche*, p. 201.
5. Wittgenstein, *Philosophical Investigations*, p. 8.
6. Ludwig Wittgenstein, *Philosophical Grammar*, ed. Rush Rhees (Oxford: Basil Blackwell, 1974), para. 55.
7. Charles Taylor, 'Theories of Meaning', *Proceedings of the British Academy*, 66 (1980), p. 327.
8. Ted Schatzki, 'Marx and Wittgenstein as Natural Historians', in Gavin Kitching and Nigel Pleasants (eds), *Marx and Wittgenstein: Knowledge, Morality and Politics* (London: Routledge, 2002), p. 55.
9. Ludwig Wittgenstein, *Remarks on Colour*, ed. G.E.M. Anscombe (Oxford: Basil Blackwell, 1977), p. 302.
10. Engels and Marx, *The German Ideology*, p. 47.
11. An excellent if somewhat exacting account of Wittgenstein's reflections on these matters is to be found in P.M.S. Hacker, *Insight and Illusion* (Oxford: Oxford University Press, 1986), esp. Ch. 7. See also G.P. Baker and P.M.S. Hacker, *Wittgenstein: Understanding and Meaning* (Oxford: Blackwell, 2005).
12. Wittgenstein, *Philosophical Investigations*, p. 46.
13. Ludwig Wittgenstein, *Remarks on the Foundations of Mathematics* (Oxford: Basil Blackwell, 1978), p. 37.
14. Wittgenstein, *Philosophical Investigations*, p. 14.

15. Quoted in J.C. Nyiri, 'Wittgenstein's Later Works in Relation to Conservatism', in Brian McGuinness (ed.), *Wittgenstein and His Times*, p. 57.

16. I have investigated this issue further in my 'Wittgenstein's Friends', in Terry Eagleton, *Against the Grain* (London: Verso, 1986), Ch. 8.

17. See Ray Monk, *Ludwig Wittgenstein: The Duty of Genius* (London: Jonathan Cape, 1990), p. 354.

18. For an account of Wittgenstein and the Soviet Union, see John Moran, 'Wittgenstein and Russia', *New Left Review*, 73 (May–June, 1972), pp. 83–96.

19. Whoever was recruiting Soviet spies at Trinity College, Cambridge did not have it all his own way. My own tutor at the college was a recruiter for British Intelligence, though he was not so rash as to try to recruit me.

20. Quoted in Maurice O'Connor Drury, 'Conversations with Wittgenstein', in Rush Rhees (ed.), *Ludwig Wittgenstein: Personal Recollections* (Oxford: Blackwell, 1981), p. 158.

21. See Norman Malcolm, *Ludwig Wittgenstein: A Memoir* (Oxford: Oxford University Press, 1958), p. 58.

22. See George Thomson, *The First Philosophers* (London: Lawrence & Wishart, 1955).

23. Wittgenstein, *Culture and Value*, p. 49.

24. McGuinness, *Wittgenstein and His Times*, p. 9.

25. See David Bloor, *Wittgenstein: A Social Theory of Knowledge* (London: Macmillan, 1983), pp. 163f.

26. For an illuminating portrait of Wittgenstein along these lines, see Neil Turnbull, 'Wittgenstein's *Leben*: Language, Philosophy and the Authority of Everyday Life', in Conor Cunningham and Peter M. Candler (eds), *Belief and Metaphysics* (London: SCM Press, 2007), pp. 374–92.

27. Merleau-Ponty, *Phenomenology of Perception*, p. 162.

28. See Wittgenstein, *Philosophical Investigations*, p. 89.

29. Fania Pascal, 'Wittgenstein: A Personal Memoir', in Rhees, *Ludwig Wittgenstein: Personal Recollections*, p. 35.

30. See Williams, *Culture and Society*, pp. 176–7, 271–2.

31. Wittgenstein, *Culture and Value*, p. 42.

32. Fergus Kerr, *Theology After Wittgenstein* (Oxford: Basil Blackwell, 1986), p. 120.

33. Jürgen Habermas, 'On Systematically Distorted Communication', *Inquiry*, 13 (1970), pp. 2015–18.

34. Georg H. von Wright, 'Wittgenstein in Relation to His Times', in McGuinness (ed.), *Wittgenstein and His Times*, p. 111.

35. Wittgenstein, *Remarks on the Foundations of Mathematics*, p. 57.

36. Wittgenstein, *Culture and Value*, p. 61.

37. See Hacker, *Insight and Illusion*, p. 233.

38. Quoted by von Wright, 'Wittgenstein in Relation to His Times', p. 113.

39. See Alice Ambrose (ed.), *Wittgenstein's Lectures: Cambridge 1932–1935* (Oxford: Blackwell, 1979), pp. 108–9.

40. Quoted by Kenny, 'Wittgenstein and the Nature of Philosophy', p. 13.

41. Quoted in Hacker, *Insight and Illusion*, p. 155. In its most degenerate form, this is known as an old-style Oxbridge tutorial.

42. Quoted by Kenny, 'Wittgenstein and the Nature of Philosophy', p. 13.

43. See Malcolm, *Ludwig Wittgenstein: A Memoir*, p. 39.

44. Wittgenstein, *Culture and Value*, p. 45.

45. Nietzsche, *Ecce Homo*, in *Basic Writings of Nietzsche*, p. 674.

46. Quoted in McGuinness (ed.), *Wittgenstein and His Times*, p. 5.

47. Ibid., p. 17.

48. See Wittgenstein, *Culture and Value*, p. 56.

49. For an original comparative study of the two philosophers, see Henry Staten, *Wittgenstein and Derrida* (Oxford: Blackwell, 1985).

50. Wittgenstein, *On Certainty*, para. 475.

51. Ibid., para. 359.

52. Kerr, *Theology After Wittgenstein*, p. 109. See also Len Doyal and Roger Harris, 'The Practical Foundations of Human Understanding', *New Left Review*, 139 (May–June, 1983), pp. 59–78, and G. Macdonald and P. Pettit, *Semantics and Social Science* (London: Routledge & Kegan Paul, 1981).

53. See Antonio Gramsci, *Selections from the Prison Notebooks*, ed. Quintin Hoare and Geoffrey Nowell Smith (London: Lawrence & Wishart, 1971), p. 330.

Index